The Besterman World Bibliographies

The Besterman World Bibliographies

Bibliography

Library Science and Reference Books

A BIBLIOGRAPHY OF BIBLIOGRAPHIES

By Theodore Besterman

TOTOWA, N. J.

Rowman and Littlefield

1971

Published by
Rowman and Littlefield
A Division of
Littlefield, Adams & Co.
81 Adams Drive
Totowa, N. J. 07512

★

Copyright © 1939, 1947, 1965, 1971
by Theodore Besterman
Printed in the United States of America

★

Typography by George Hornby
and Theodore Besterman

ISBN 0-87471-041-3

Contents

Preface

I have explained in the Introduction to the successive editions of *A World bibliography of bibliographies* why I decided to arrange it alphabetically by specific subjects. Since that decision was taken, and after prolonged experience of the book in use, I have had no reason to regret it, nor among the many letters I have received from librarians has there been a single one complaining of the alphabetical form of the *World bibliography*.

The *World bibliography of bibliographies* covers all subjects and all languages, and is intended to serve reference and research purposes of the most specific and specialised kind. Yet contained in it are broad and detailed surveys which, if relevant entries throughout the volumes are added to them, can serve also the widest reference inquiries, and be useful to those who seek primary signposts to information in varied fields of inquiry.

Therefore I can only thank Rowman and Littlefield for having gathered together all the titles in some of the major fields found throughout the 6664 columns of the fourth edition (1965-1966) of *A World bibliography of bibliographies*.

Preface

These fields are:

1. Bibliography
2. Printing
3. Periodical Publications
4. Academic Writings
5. Art and Architecture
6. Music and Drama
7. Education
8. Agriculture
9. Medicine
10. Law
11. English and American Literature
12. Technology
13. Physical Sciences
14. Biological Sciences
15. Family History
16. Commerce, Manufactures, Labour
17. History
18. Geography

Of course these categories by no means exhaust the 117,000 separately collated volumes set out in the *World bibliography,* and the above titles will be added to if librarians wish for it.

Th. B.

Notes on the Arrangement

An Alternative to critical annotation

Consider what it is we look for in a normal bibliography of a special subject. Reflection will show, I think, that we look, above all, for completeness, just as we do in a bibliography of bibliographies. We desire completeness even more than accuracy (painfully uncongenial though it is for me to make such a statement); for in most cases a bibliography is intended to give us particulars of publications to which we wish to refer; thus we can always judge for ourselves (waiving gross errors) whether the bibliographer has correctly described these publications. On the other hand, anything that is omitted is lost until rediscovered.

The question is, therefore, whether it is possible to give some indication of the degree of completeness of a bibliography without indulging in the annotation which is impossible in a work of the present scope and scale. It seemed to me that this could be achieved, to a considerable extent, by recording the approximate number of entries set out in it. This method is, of course, a rough-and-ready one, but experience shows that it is remarkably effective: and I hope that its novelty will not tell against it.

The recording of the number of works set out in a bibliography has another advantage in the case of serial publications: it displays in statistical form the development of the subject from year to year—often in a highly significant manner.

This procedure, then, is that which I have adopted, the number of items in each bibliography being shown in square brackets at the end of the entry. This, I may add, is by no means an easy or mechanical task, as can be judged from the fact that this process, on the average, just about doubles the time taken in entering each bibliography.

Supplementary information in footnotes

I have said that this method of indicating the number of entries is intended to replace critical treatment; but it is not possible to exclude annotation altogether, for a certain minimum of added information is indispensable. Consequently many of my entries will be seen to have footnotes, in which the following types of information are recorded: a few words of explanation where the title is inaccurate, misleading, obscure, or insufficiently informative; a statement to that effect where a work is in progress, where intermediate volumes in a series have not been published, or where no more have been published; an attempt to clarify complicated series; a note that a book was privately printed or in a limited number of copies, where this does not exceed 500, or in some abnormal manner, as on one side of the leaf, on coloured paper, or in a reproduction of hand-writing, or with erratic pagination; when I have come across copies containing manuscript or other added matter, I have recorded the fact; substantial corrections and additions to bibliographies are sometimes published in periodicals, and I have noted a good many of these—but without aiming at anything even remotely approaching completeness, the attainment of which would be impossible. Various minor types of information are also occasionally to be found in the footnotes.

Owing to the great increase in the number of bibliographies reproduced directly from type-written copy, such publications are designated by an asterisk at the end of the entry; this device saves a good deal of space.

Place of publication

The place of publication is not shown when it is London in the case of an english book and

Notes

Paris in the case of a french one. In the case of a series or sequence of entries, however, the absence of a place of publication means that it is the same as the place last shown in the series. The same applies to the names of editors and compilers. The place of publication is given as it appears on the titlepage, but prepositions are omitted even if violence is done to grammatical construction.

The Order of entries

Under each heading the order of the entries is chronological by date of publication; in the case of works in successive volumes or editions the chronological order applies to the first volume or edition. In suitable long headings an additional chronological order by period covered has been created; see, for instance, France: History, or Drama: Great Britain.

Method of collating

An effort has been made, so far as space allows, to give detailed and accurate information of the kind more usually found in small bibliographies. For instance, I have paid special attention to the collation of bibliographies in several (or even numerous) parts or volumes. It is, in fact, difficult to understand why it is usually considered necessary to give collations of works in a single volume,

Notes

where difficulties seldom occur (from the point of view of systematic bibliography), but not of a work in several volumes, where confusion much more frequently arises. An occasional gap in the collations of such publications will be noticed. This is because, naturally enough, I have not been able in every case to see perfect sets; and I have thought it better to leave a very small number of such blanks rather than to hold up the bibliography indefinitely.

Serial publications

Where successive issues of a serial publication are set out, the year or period shown is usually that covered by the relevant issue; in such cases no date of publication is given unless publication was abnormal or erratic in relation to the period covered.

Bibliographies in more than one edition

Where a bibliography has gone into more than one edition I have tried (though I have not always been able) to record at least the first and latest editions. Intermediate editions have also been recorded wherever it seemed useful to do so, that is, for bibliographies first published before 1800, and for those of special interest or importance; but in general intermediate editions, though examined, have not been recorded.

Notes

Transcription of titles

Titles have been set out in the shortest possible form consistent with intelligibility and an adequate indication of the scope of the bibliography; omissions have of course been indicated. The author's name, generally speaking, is given as it appears on the titlepage, amplified and interpreted within square brackets where necessary.

Anonymous bibliographies

Far too large a proportion of bibliographical work is published anonymously. This is due, in part, to the all too common practice of library committees and similar bodies of suppressing altogether or of hiding in prefaces the names of those who have compiled bibliographies and catalogues for them. I have spent a good deal of time in excavating such and other evidences of authorship, and the result may be seen in the large number of titles preceded by names enclosed within square brackets.

Th. B.

Bibliography.

I

Bibliography

1. Bibliographies of bibliographies and of bibliography

AKSEL G[USTAV] S[ALOMON] JOSEPHSON, Bibliographies of bibliographies chronologically arranged. Bibliographical society of Chicago: Contributions to bibliography (vol.i): Chicago 1901. pp.47. [157.]

500 copies printed; a supplement by [Gustaf] V[ilhelm] Grundtvig appears in the Centralblatt für bibliothekswesen *(1903), xx.432–438; and a second edition of the original work in the* Bulletin *of the Bibliographical society of America (1910), ii.21–24, 54–56; (1911), iii.23–24, 50–53; (1912), iv.23–27, and the same body's* Papers *(1912–1913), vii.115–124.*

PHILIPPE LABBÉ, Bibliotheca bibliothecarvm, cvris secvndis avctior. Accedit bibliotheca nvmmaria. Parisiis 1664. pp.[xxvii].394. [bibliographies: 1500.]

— — Editio secundo auctior. Rothomagi 1672, pp.[xxxii].398. [1500.]

— — Editio III. 1678. pp.[xxxii].398+27 [1500.]

— — Editio IV. Lipsiæ 1682. pp.[lxxii].671+38. [1500.]

first issued as a Specimen *in 1653.*

Bibliography

VALENTINUS HENRICUS VOGLERUS, Introdvctio vniversalis in notitiam cvivscvnque generis bonorvm scriptorvm. Helmestadii 1670. pp.[xvi].114. [xiv]. [250.]

ANTOINE TEISSIER, Catalogus avctorvm qvi librorvm catalogos, indices, bibliothecas, virorum litteratorum elogia, vitas, aut orationes funebres, scriptis consignârunt. Genevæ 1686. pp.[vii].559. [3000.]
—— Catalogi auctorum qvi librorum catalogos . . . scriptis consignârunt auctuarium . . . sive ejusdem catalogi pars altera. 1705. pp.[v].368.27. [iii]. [3000.]

JOHANN JUSTUS VON EINEM, Succincta in bibliothecam historiæ litterariæ introductio. Magdeburgi 1738. pp.158. [750.]

[JACQUES BERNARD DUREY DE NOINVILLE], Dissertation sur les bibliothèques, avec une table alphabétique, tant des ouvrages publiés sous le titre de Bibliothèques, que des catalogues imprimés de plusieurs cabinets de France & des pays étrangers. 1758. pp.[v].156.[iii]. [750.]
one of the Bibliothèque nationale copies contains ms. notes.

3

[ÉTIENNE] GABRIEL PEIGNOT, Répertoire bibliographique universel, contenant la notice raisonnée
des bibliographies spéciales . . . d'autres ouvrages
de bibliographie, relatifs à l'histoire littéraire, et à
toutes les parties de la bibliographie. 1812. pp.xx.
514. [2000.]

THOMAS HARTWELL HORNE, An introduction to
the study of bibliography. 1814. pp.xvi.402+[iv].
403-759.clvi. [1000.]
*the text of the second volume consists of 'A notice of
the principal works, extant on literary history in general
and on bibliography in particular.'*

[JEAN] P[IE] NAMUR, Bibliographie paléogra-
phico-diplomatico-bibliologique. Liége 1838. pp.
xxvii.227+vi.306. [10,236.]

ANZEIGER für literatur der bibliothekswissen-
schaft [*afterwards:* für bibliographie und biblio-
thekswissenschaft]. [Edited by Julius Petzholdt.]
Dresden &c. 1840-1855.
details of this work are given under Libraries, below.

F[REDERIK] MULLER, Catalogus van de bibliotheek der Vereeniging ter bevordering van de
belangen des boekhandels. Amsterdam 1855. pp.
xvi.144. [bibliography: 938.]
—— [another edition]. 's-Gravenhage 1920–

1934. pp.xvi.484 + xii.485–837 + xvi.839–1095. cxli.13+xvi.590. [45,000.]

—— Aanvulling.

   1927.
   1928. pp.71. [850.]
   1929. pp.38. [450.]
   1930. pp.42. [500.]
   1931. pp.41. [500.]
   1932.
   1933. pp.43. [500.]
   1934–1935. pp.80. [1000.]

CATALOGUE of the books on bibliography, typography and engraving, in the New-York state library. Albany 1858. pp.3–143. [1250.]

REUBEN A[LDRIDGE] GUILD, The librarian's manual; a treatise on bibliography, comprising a select and descriptive list of bibliographical works. New York 1858. pp.10.304. [750.]
500 copies printed.

JULIUS PETZHOLDT, Bibliotheca bibliographica. Kritisches verzeichniss der das gesammtgebiet der bibliographie betreffenden litteratur des in- und auslandes. Leipzig 1866. pp.xii.939. [5500.]
a facsimile reprint was published in 1961.

JOSEPH SABIN, A bibliography of bibliography,

or a handy book about books which relate to books. New York 1877. pp.v–cl. [1000.]

[LÉON] GAUDIN, Catalogue de la Bibliothèque de la ville de Montpellier . . . Histoire littéraire et bibliographie. Montpellier 1878. pp.xv.190. [687.]

GUSTAVE PAWLOWSKI, Les travaux bibliographiques de 1867 à 1878 Société bibliographique: 1879. pp.80. [400.]
200 copies printed.

J. D. O., Some french bibliographies. 1881. pp. [iv].87. [400.]
160 copies printed.

[GEORGE WILLIAM PORTER], Hand-list of bibliographies, classified catalogues, and indexes placed in the Reading room of the British museum for reference. 1881. pp.106. [1250.]
— — List of bibliographical works in the Reading room of the British museum. Second edition, revised [by George Knottesford Fortescue]. 1889. pp.xi.104. [1000.]

LÉON VALLÉE, Bibliographie des bibliographies. 1883. pp.vii.774. [6894.]
— — Supplément. 1887. pp.[iii].355. [3352.]

WILLIAM COOLIDGE LANE, Index to recent reference lists. Harvard university: Library: Bibliogra-

phical contributions (no.20&c.): Cambridge, Mass.
   [i]. 1884–1885 . . . (no.20): 1885. pp.[ii].8.
   [400.]
   [ii]. 1885–1886 . . . (no.24): 1887. pp.9. [300.]
   iii. 1887 . . . (no.29): 1888. pp.11. [400.]
   iv. 1888–1890 . . . (no.40): 1891. pp.25. [950.]

[FRÉDÉRIC ALEXANDRE] HENRI STEIN, Les travaux
bibliographiques de 1878 à 1888. Congrès bibliographique international . . . 1888: 1889. pp.104.
[1000.]

JAMES LYMAN WHITNEY, A catalogue of the
bibliographies of special subjects in the Boston
public library. Public library: Bibliographies of
special subjects (no.5): Boston 1890. pp.[ii].71.
[3500.]

J[OHN] POTTER BRISCOE and PAUL HERRING, Bibliography. Public reference library: Class list
(no.15): Nottingham 1890. pp.16. [400.]

PAUL BERGMANS, Répertoire méthodique décen-
nal des travaux bibliographiques parus en Belgique. 1881–1890. Liége 1892. pp.76. [369.]
100 copies printed.

CATALOGO di opere biografiche e bibliografiche
raccolte dal dott. Diamede Bonamici. Lucca 1893.
pp.[v].228. [2250.]

[FRÉDÉRIC ALEXANDRE] HENRI STEIN, Manuel de bibliographie générale. Manuels de bibliographie historique (vol.ii): 1897 [*on cover:* 1898]. pp.xx. 895. [5500.]
a facsimile was published New York 1962.

БИБЛІОГРАФИЧЕСКІЕ матеріалы. Опись книгъ, брошюръ и статей библіотеки сенатора Н. П. Смирнова [Nikolai Pavlovich Smirnov]. Санкт-Петербургъ 1898. pp.xvi.690.ii. [5000.]

ALICE NEWMAN, Index to subject bibliographies in library bulletins to December 31, 1897. University of the state of New York: State library bulletin (Bibliography no.14): Albany 1898. pp.369–426. [1250.]

H[ENRY] LA FONTAINE, Bibliographia universalis. . . . Bibliographia economica universalis. Répertoire annuel des travaux de bibliographie. Institut International de Bibliographie (Contribution no.31): Bruxelles.
    i. 1898. 1900. ff.3–73. [553.]
    ii. 1899. 1900. pp.8.ff.9–73.pp.75–84. [512.]
    iii. 1900. 1902. pp.8.ff.9–92.pp.93–108. [650.]
    iv. 1901. 1903. pp.9.ff.11–66.pp.67–86. [431.]
    v. 1902. 1904. pp.xiv.ff.112.pp.113–140. [814.]

vi. 1903. 1906. pp.xii.ff.100.pp.101–107.[645.]
no more published.

JOHN FERGUSON, Some aspects of bibliography.
Edinburgh 1900. pp.[vii].103. [452.]

ANDREW KEOGH, Some general bibliographical
works of value to the student of english. Yale
University: [New Haven] 1901. pp.28. [150.]
printed on one side of the leaf.

A LIST of bibliographies of special subjects. John
Crerar library: Chicago 1902. pp.504. [2000.]

CATALOGUS der bibliographie en bibliotheconomie. Koninklijke bibliotheek: [The Hague] 1903.
pp.[iii].76. [2405.]

TORSTEIN [KNUTSON TORSTENSEN-] JAHR and
ADAM JULIUS STROHM, Bibliography of coopera-
tive cataloguing and the printing of catalogue
cards, with incidental references to international
bibliography and the universal catalogue. Washington 1903. pp.116. [366.]

D. V. ULYANINSKY, Среди книгъ и ихъ
друзей . . . Русскія книжныя росписи XVIII
вѣка. Москва 1903. pp.[vii].138. [128.]
325 copies printed.

Bibliography

BIBLIOGRAPHIE des bibliotheks- und buchwesens. Zentralblatt für bibliothekswesen: Beiheft (no. xxix &c.): Leipzig.

> 1904. Bearbeitet von Adalbert Hortzschansky ... (no.xxix): 1905. pp.134. [1621.]
>
> 1905 ... (no.xxxi): 1906. pp.viii.144. [1679.]
>
> 1906 ... (no.xxxii): 1907. pp.ix.160. [1846.]
>
> 1907 ... (no.xxxiv): 1908. pp.ix.172. [1991.]
>
> 1908 ... (no.xxxvi): 1909. pp.vii.159. [1791.]
>
> 1909 ... (no.xxxvii): 1910. pp.vii.144. [1636.]
>
> 1910 ... (no.xxxix): 1911. pp.vii.136. [1579.]
>
> 1911 ... (no.xl): 1912. pp.vii.152. [1787.]
>
> 1912 ...(no.xlii): 1913. pp.vii.150. [1860.]
>
> 1922. Bearbeitet von Richard Meckelein ... (no.li): 1923. pp.vii.116. [1750.]
>
> 1923 ... (no.54): 1925. pp.[vi].166. [2250.]
>
> 1924. Von R. Hoecker ... (no.56): 1926. pp.[v].240. [3500.]
>
> 1925. Bearbeitet von Rudolf Hoecker und Joris Vorstius ... (no.58): 1927. pp.vii.408. [6000.]

[*continued as:*]

Internationale bibliographie des buch- und bibliothekswesens, mit besonderer berücksichtigung der bibliographie. Neue folge.

> i. 1926. Bearbeitet von R. Hoecker und J.

Bibliography

Vorstius. 1928. pp.viii.130. [3500.]

ii. 1927. 1928. pp.viii.146. [4000.]

iii. 1928. 1929. pp.viii.203. [5500.]

iv. 1929. 1930. pp.viii.199. [6000.]

v. 1930. In kritischer auswahl zusammengestellt von J. Vorstius und Erwin Steinborn.
1931. pp.xi.224. [7500.]

vi. 1931. 1932. pp.xii.coll.332. [5500.]

vii. 1932. 1933. pp.xii.coll.370. [6000.]

viii. 1933. 1934. pp.xii.coll.370. [6000.]

ix. 1934. In kritischer auswahl zusammengestellt von J. Vorstius und Gerhard Reincke.
1935. pp.x.coll.416. [6500.]

x. 1935. [1936]. pp.xii.coll.394. [6000.]

xi. 1936. 1937. pp.x.coll.394. [6000.]

xii. 1937. 1938. pp.xii.coll.450. [6500.]

xiii. 1938. 1939. pp.xii.coll.438. [6500.]

xiv. 1939. 1940. pp.xii.coll.384. [6000.]

xv. 1940. Zusammengestellt von J. Vorstius
und Erwin Steinborn. 1941. pp.xii.coll.533.
[7500.]

not published for 1913–1921.

WILLIAM PRIDEAUX COURTNEY, A register of national bibliography, with a selection of the chief
bibliographical books and articles printed in other

countries. 1905–1912. pp.iii–viii.314+[iv].315–631+v.340. [30,000].

JAMES DOUGLAS STEWART and OLIVE E. CLARKE, Book selection. 1909. pp.16. [97.]

G[ERRIT] A[LBERT] EVERS, Nederlandsche bibliografie van boek- en bibliotheekwezen. Centrale vereeniging voor openbare leeszalen en bibliotheken: 's-Gravenhage [Utrecht].

    1910. pp.40.
    1911. pp.52.

BIBLIOGRAPHIES contributed by the Library to publications of other departments or institutions. Library of Congress: Washington 1913. ff.6. [21.]*

REGINALD G. WILLIAMS, A manual of book selection for the librarian and book-lover. 1920. pp. [iv].132. [1000.]

GIUSEPPE FAMAGALLI, La bibliografia. Guide bibliografiche: Roma 1923. pp.lxxxix.169. [1039.]

[EDMUND] GEORG SCHNEIDER, Handbuch der bibliographie. Leipzig 1923. pp.xvi.544. [2500.]
    — — Vierte . . . auflage. Leipzig 1930. pp.ix. 676. [5500.]

A[UGUSTA] V[LADIMIROVNA] MEZIER, Словарный

указатель по книговедению. Ленинград 1924. pp.xi.coll.926. pp.viii. [10,000.]

STANISŁAW PIOTR KOCZOROWSKI, Coup d'œil sur l'histoire de bibliographie en Pologne. 1924. pp. 26. [20.]
100 copies printed; reprinted in 1925 as a so-called 'nouvelle édition'.

LITERARISCHES beiblatt der Zeitschrift [*afterwards:* zum Jahrbuch] des Deutschen vereins für buchwesen und schrifttum. Leipzig.
  i. 1924. Schriftleitung: Hans H. Bockwitz. pp.19.20.18. [1000.]
  ii. 1925. pp.20.19.16.23. [1500.]
  iii. 1926. pp.16.31.26. [1500.]
  iv. 1927. pp.20.19.16. [1000.]
  v. 1928. pp.18.16.24. [1000.]
  vi. 1929. pp.26.20.22. [1000.]
  vii. 1930. pp.21.19.24. [1000.]
  viii. 1931. pp.25.18. [500.]
  ix. 1932. pp.18.11. [250.]
  x. 1933. pp.18.9. [250.]
  xi. 1934. pp.21.10. [250.]
  xii. 1935. pp.16.16. [500.]
  xiii. 1936. pp.14. [500.]

MARCEL GODET, Index bibliographicus. Répertoire international des sources de bibliographie courante (périodiques et institutions). Société des nations: Commission de coopération intellectuelle: Genève 1925. pp.xvi.233. [1002.]

— — Zweite . . . Auflage. Herausgegeben von M. Godet & Joris Vorstius. Berlin &c. 1931. pp. xxiii.420. [1900.]

[—] — Third edition. Compiled by Theodore [Deodatus Nathaniel] Besterman. Unesco [United nations educational, scientific and cultural organization] &c.: Paris 1952.

    i. Science and technology. pp.xi.52. [1250.]

    ii. Social sciences, education, humanistic studies. pp.xi.72. [1750.]

[—] — 4th edition. Fédération internationale de documentation: La Haye.

    i. Science and technology. 1959. pp.[vi].119. [2000.]

in progress?

TITLES of lists of books, or bibliographies, which have been distributed, or which are in course of preparation. National book council: 1927. pp.[4]. [105.]

        [continued as:]
Subject index of book lists.

    February 1928. pp.[4]. [115.]

    September 1928. pp.[4]. [123.]

1930. pp.6. [130.]
1931. pp.6. [135.]
1935. pp.8. [145.]
1936. pp.8. [148.]

BIBLJOGRAFIA [Bibliografia] bibljografji, biblijo-
tekarstwa i biblojofilstwa. Przegląd biblioteczny:
Dodatek: Kraków.

    1928. [By] Władysław Tadeusz Wisłocki.
      pp.[ii].92. [1530.]
    1929.
    1930. [By] M[arja] Mazankówna-Friedber-
      gowa. pp.[ii].58.10. [868.]
    1931. pp.46. [594.]
    1932. pp.19. [392.]
    1933. pp.22. [440.]
    1934. pp.32. [661.]
    1935-1936. [By] Wanda Żurowska. pp.65.
      [1371.]

no more published.

HENRY BARTLETT VAN HOESEN and FRANK KELLER
WALTER, Bibliography: practical, enumerative,
historical. New York &c. 1929. pp.xvi.519. [1250.]

M. N. KUFAEV, Теория библиографии. Указатель литературы за десять лет. 1917-1927.
Москва 1928. pp.43. [322.]

BIBLIOGRAFIA italiana. . . . Gruppo H. Bibliografia e biografie. Consiglio nazionale delle ricerche: Bologna.

> 1929. 1930. pp.[v].86. [1611.]
> *no more published.*

GIANETTO AVANZI, Catalogo dei libri e periodici esposti nelle sezione "bibliografia". Primo Congresso mondiale delle biblioteche e di bibliografia: Roma [1930]. pp.119. [533.]

JORIS VORSTIUS, Kritischer überblick über die bibliographische literatur des jahres 1929. Linz a. Donau 1931. pp.31. [200.]

INTERNATIONALER jahresbericht der bibliographie. Leipzig.

> i. 1930. Herausgegeben von Joris Vorstius. pp.vii.56. [249.]
> ii. 1931. pp.[vii].52. [209.]
> iii. 1932. pp[vii].64. [250.]
> iv. 1933. pp.vi.48. [194.]
> v. 1934. pp.vi.38. [232.]
> vi. 1935. pp.vi.41. [165.]
> vii. 1936. pp.vi.46. [194.]
> viii. 1937. pp.[v].44. [162.]
> ix. 1938. pp.[v].46. [170.]
> x. 1939. pp.[v].36. [167.]
> xi. 1940. pp.[v].44. [165.]

Bibliography

GEORGE WATSON COLE, An index to bibliographical papers published by the Bibliographical society and the Library association, London, 1877–1932. Bibliographical society of America: Chicago [printed] 1933. pp.ix.262. [3750.]

LIJST van boeken en tijdschriftartikelen van nederlandsche schrijvers over documentatie. Nederlandsch instituut voor documentatie en registratuur: Publicatie (no.85): Purmerend 1933. ff.[i].16. [250.]

BOOKS about books. A catalogue of the books contained in the National book council library. 1933. pp.48. [500.]
— — [Fourth edition]. Catalogue of the library of the National book council. 1944. pp.64. [1200.]

[GUSTAF] VIHELM GRUNDTVIG, Inledning til bibliografien. København 1935. pp.34. [125.]

THEODORE [DEODATUS NATHANIEL] BESTERMAN, The beginnings of systematic bibliography. [Oxford books on bibliography:] 1935. pp.xi.83. [250.]
— — Second edition. 1936. pp.xi.82. [250.]
this edition was reprinted in 1950.
— — Troisième édition. Les débuts de la bibliographie méthodique. 1950. pp.3–99. [300.]

17

a facsimile of this edition was issued, New York
1960.

WINSLOW L. WEBBER, Books about books.
Boston 1937. pp.[vii].168. [1000.]
not limited to books.

BULLETIN de documentation bibliographique.
Bibliothèque nationale [and Union française des
organismes de documentation].★
    iv. 1937–1938. ff.[i].205. [1770.]
    v. 1938. ff.206. [1177.]
    vi. 1939. ff.130. [849.]
    vii. 1940. ff.138. [986.]
    viii. 1941. ff.106. [580.]
    ix. 1942. ff.136. [679.]
    x. 1943. ff.189. [1343.]
    xi. 1944. ff.137. [1091.]
    xii. 1945. ff.82. [700.]
    xiii. 1946. ff.306. [2414.]
    xiv. 1947. ff.273. [2015.]
    xv. 1948. ff.291. [2190.]
    xvi. 1949. ff.298. [2339.]
    xvii. 1950. ff.249. [1937.]
    xviii. 1951. ff.377. [3054.]
    xix. 1952. ff.456.
    xx. 1953. ff.438. [2881.]
    xxi. 1954. pp.363. [2365.]
    xxii. 1955. pp.438. [3541.]

earlier issues form part of the Bulletin mensuel de l'Union française des organismes de documentation *and later ones of the* Bulletin des bibliothèques de France.

UNION list of literature on library science and bibliography up to 1935. League of young librarians: Osaka 1938. pp.260. [2375.]

THE BIBLIOGRAPHIC index. A cumulative bibliography of bibliographies. New York.

> i. 1937–1942. Edited by Dorothy Charles and Bea Joseph. 1945. pp.xxiii.1780. [50,000.]
>
> ii. 1943–1946. Edited by Helen T. Geer. pp. xx.831. [20,000.]
>
> iii. 1947–1950. pp.xvii.796. [20,000.]
>
> iv. 1951–1955. Edited by Marga Franck. pp. xii.709. [20,000.]
>
> v. 1956–1959. pp.xvi.801. [25,000.]

in progress; only the final cumulated editions are listed.

WILHELM KRABBE, Bibliographie. Ein hilfsbuch für bibliothekspraktikanten. 3. . . . Auflage. Veröffentlichungen der Berliner bibliothekschule (no.i): Leipzig 1939. pp.66. [400.]

— — 6. . . . auflage. Hamburg 1951. pp.102. [500.]

THEODORE [DEODATUS NATHANIEL] BESTERMAN, A world bibliography of bibliographies. 1939–

1940. pp.xxiv.588+[iv].644. [25,000.]
privately printed.

— — Second edition. 1947–1949. pp.xxviii.
coll.1452 + pp.[iv].coll.1451–3198 + pp.[vi].coll.
3197–4114. [40,000.]
privately printed; the second edition reprinted in 1950.

— — Third ... edition. Societas bibliographica:
Genève 1955–1956. pp.xxviii.coll.1326+pp.[iv].
coll.1327–2858 + pp.[v].coll.2859–4408 + pp.[v].
coll.4409–5701. [60,000.]
reprinted in 1960 in reduced facsimile.

HANS BOHATTA and FRANZ HODES, Internationale
bibliographie der bibliographien. Frankfurt am
Main [1939–1950]. pp.[vi].652. [16,000.]
*on the titlepage the authors are given as above, 'unter
mitwirkung von Walter Funke'; on the covers of the
first four parts the work is shown as by Bohatta and
Funke.*

[GIANETTO AVANZI], La bibliografia italiana. Istituto nazionale per le relazioni culturali con l'estero:
Bibliografie del ventennio: Roma 1941. pp.xviii.
248. [679.]

T[ODOR] BOROV, Пжтя къмъ книгитѣ. Уводъ
въ библиографията. Български библиогра-

фски институтъ (no.3): София 1942. pp.viii.157. [500.]

REGISTER op de noord- en zuidnederlandsche bibliographische tijdschriften. Het boeck (new ser., vol.xxvii): Den Haag 1943. pp.viii.317.

KNUD LARSEN, Boghandelens bibliografi, med en fortegnelse over danske bibliografier ved Arne J. Møller. København 1943. pp.134. [500.]
—— [another edition]. 1951. pp.141. [750.]

ВАЖНЕЙШИЕ библиографические работы библиотек. Государственная библиотека СССР им. В. И. Ленина: Москва.

    i. 1943. pp.26. [365.]
    ii. 1943. pp.30. [380.]
    iii. 1943. pp.20. [186.]
    iv. 1943. pp.16. [198.]
    v. 1943. pp.24. [343.]
    vi. 1944. pp.26. [358.]
    vii. 1944. pp.20. [318.]
    viii. 1944. pp.20. [289.]
    ix. 1944. pp.20. [280.]
    x. 1944. pp.24. [378.]
no more published?

W[ILHELM] P[REUS] SOMMERFELDT, Norks bibliografisk litteratur 1919–1944. Oslo 1944. pp.42. [750.]

Bibliography

ARCHER TAYLOR, Renaissance guides to books. Berkeley &c. 1945. pp.[vii].130. [150.]

NORMA OLIN IRELAND, *ed.* Local indexes in american libraries. A union list of unpublished indexes. Useful reference series (no.73): Boston 1947. pp.xxxv.221. [8000.]

JORGE AGUAYO, Lista de obras de bibliotecología y bibliografía existentes en la biblioteca general de la universidad. La Habana 1948. ff.[ii].19. [292.]*

LIST of bibliographies compiled by the Division of bibliography fiscal years 1936–1947. Library of Congress: Washington 1948. ff.9. [278.]*

FRANK SEYMOUR SMITH, Pamphlet bibliographies. National book league: Reader's guide: 1948. pp.24. [125.]
the title is misleading; this purports to be a select list of bibliographies in pamphlet form.

MARIA DEMBOWSKA, Bibliografia bibliografii i nauki o książce. Biblioteka narodowa: Warszawa 1948 &c.

BIBLIOGRAFÍA de bibliografías y biblioteconomía 1936–1948. Universidad nacional mayor de San Marcos: Biblioteca central: Lima 1949. pp.28. [369.]

Bibliography

JOAN M[ARY] HARRIES, Union list of bibliographies. A selection of . . . bibliographies with locations in some metropolitan & greater London libraries. Association of assistant librarians: Greater London division: 1950. pp.53. [400.]

— — [another edition]. Reference books and bibliographies. A union list. By L[eonard] M[aslin] Payne and J. M. Harries. 1957. pp.xii.92. [800.]★

this is a conflation of the Union list *and the work entered under Reference books, 1954.*

ROBERT L[EWIS WRIGHT] COLLISON, Bibliographies, subject and national. 1951. pp.xii.172. [500.]

K[URT] FLEISCHHACK, Leitfaden der bibliographie, mit einer auswahl-bibliographie der bibliographie. Heidelberg 1951. pp.80. [250.]

L[ONARD] M[ASLIN] PAYNE and E[DWARD] P[ERRY] DUDLEY, A select list of reference books and bibliographies for the use of students preparing for . . . examinations of the Library association. [Second edition]. North-western polytechnic: Department of librarianship: 1951. pp.50. [561.]

LITERATURVERZEICHNIS zur dokumentation. Handbücher der klassifikation (no.1 &c.): Berlin [1951 &c.: Stuttgart].

1930–1950. Von Otto Frank. . . . (no.7): pp.
156. [1300.]

1951–1954. . . . (no.10). pp.119. [900.]

1955–1958. . . . (no.11). pp.141. [1200.]
in progress.

LIST of bibliographies and theses accepted for
part III of the university of London diploma in
librarianship between 1936 and 1950. University
of London: School of librarianship and archives:
Occasional publications (no.1): 1951. pp.10. [150.]★
— [another edition]. Cumulated list of bibliographies and theses accepted for part II . . . 1946–
1960. . . . (no.10): 1960. pp.[iv].37. [299.]★

BIBLIOGRAPHIE de la documentation et de la
bibliothéconomie. Fédération internationale de
documentation: Publication (no.260 &c.): La
Haye.

1951. . . . (no.260). pp.36. [491.]

1952. . . . (no.262). pp.54. [713.]

1953.

1954. . . . (no.276). pp.52. [508.]

1955. . . . (no.291). pp.72. [803.]

1956. . . . (no.299). pp.59. [655.]

1957. . . . (no.309). pp.67. [861.]

1958. . . . (no.319). pp.42. [537.]

1959. . . . (no.326). pp.38. [357.]

1960. . . . (no.332). pp.48. [503.]
1961. . . . (no.341). pp.36. [360.]
in progress.

ABSTRACTS, bibliographies and indexes at the Howard college library. Durban 1952. pp.26. [300.]*

J[ULIEN] VAN HOVE, La bibliographie en Belgique en 1951. Commission belge de bibliographie: Publications (no.1): [Bruxelles 1952]. pp.13. [100.]*

ITALIA bibliographica. Repertorio delle opere di bibliografia . . . apparse in opere e in periodici stampati in Italia. "Amor di libro" (vol.xii &c.): Firenze.

1952. [By] Giuseppe Sergio Martini. . . . (vol. xv). pp.128. [300.]

1953. pp.95. [200.]

1954. . . . (vol.xviii). pp.93. [200.]

1955. . . . (vol.xx). pp.26. [300.]

1956. . . . (vol.xxiv). pp.102. [250.]

1957.

1958. [By] Bona Edlmann. . . . (vol.xxxi). pp.118. [300.]

1959. . . . (vol.xxxiv). pp.125. [300.]

in progress; 333 copies printed.

Bibliography

JÓZEF GRYCZ and EMILIA KURDYBACHA, Bibliografia w teorii i praktyce oraz wykaz ważniejszych bibliografij i dzieł pomocniczych. Warszawa 1953. pp.216. [300.]

LOUISE NOËLLE MALCLÈS, Cours de bibliographie à l'intention des étudiants de l'université et des candidats aux examens de bibliothécaire. Genève &c. 1954. pp.xii.350. [2000.]

HANDLIST of bibliographies on exhibition at the Hastings conference. Library association: London and home counties branch: [Eastbourne 1954]. pp.32 [661.]*

WILHELM TOTOK and ROLF WEITZEL, Handbuch der bibliographischen nachschlagewerke. Frankfurt am Main 1954. pp.xxii.258. [2000.]
—— Zweite . . . auflage. [1959]. pp.xvi.335. [2500.]

БИБЛИОГРАФИЯ советской библиографии. Всесоюзная книжная палата: Москва.
    1954. pp.271. [4164].
    1955. pp.314. [4857.]
    1956. pp.367. [5865.]
    1957. pp.374. [6559.]
    1958. pp.[ii].lxiii.416. [6987.]
    1959. pp.xcii.510. [8613.]

1960. pp.lxxx.512. [8669.]
1961. pp.lxxxiv.532. [9067.]
1962. pp.lxxx.420. [8576.]
in progress.

ERWIN FELKEL, Repertorio dei prezzi delle opere di bibliografia nel 1952. Volume primo [–terzo]. A-C [–Q]. "Amor di libro" (vols.xvi, xxii,): Firenze 1954–1958. pp.136+150+134. [2500.]
333 copies printed; no more published.

S. T. H. WRIGHT and I. MCKINLAY, A classified list of catalogues and bibliographies in the library. Scottish central library: Edinburgh 1955. pp.iv.63. [665.]*

[M. A. ANDREEVA and M. K. DERUNOVA], Общая библиография. Методические указания для студентов заочных отделений библиотечных институтов. Управление учебных заведений: Москва 1955. pp.48. [150.]

[JOZEF KUZMIK], Le passé et l'état actuel de la bibliographie slovaque. Bibliothèque nationale slovaque "Matica slovenska": Martin 1955. pp.10. [100.]

BIBLIOGRAFÍA bibliotecológica colombiana. Manuales de bibliografía y documentación colombianas (no.1): Bogotá.

Bibliography

1953–1955. Recogida por Luis Florén. pp.57. [381.]

[*continued as:*]

Bibliografía bibliotecológica y bibliográfica colombiana.

1956–1958. pp.[vii].35. [235.]*

GILBER VARET, Histoire et savoir. Introduction théorique à la bibliographie. Les champs articulés de la bibliographie philosophique. Université de Besançon: Annales littéraires (vol.12): Paris 1956· pp.225. [600.]

MILOŠ PAPÍRNÍK, Soupis zahraničních neperiodiských bibliografií ve státních vědeckých knihovnách a vysokoskolských knihovnách. Universita: Knihovna: Na pomoc knihovníkům a čtenérům (no.10): Brně 1956. pp.[ii].vi.48. [400.]*

A LIST of checklists used in surveys of library book collections. Committee for the protection of cultural and scientific resources: Washington 1956. pp.18. [151.]*

W[ILFRED] L[EONARD] SAUNDERS, A guide to book lists and bibliographies for the use of school librarians. School library association: 1956. pp.ii. 30. [306.]
— 2nd edition. 1961. pp.iv.40. [557.]

LOUISE NOËLLE MALCLÈS, La bibliographie. "Que sais-je?" [no.708]: 1956. pp.136. [700.]

—— Deuxième édition. 1962. pp.136. [700.]

SOUPIS českých bibliografií. Bibliograficky katalog ČSR: Ceské knihy: Praha.

    i. 1956. Zpracovala Saša Mouchová. pp.60. [1160.]

    ii. 1957. pp.72. [1332.]

    iii. 1958. pp.80. [1597.]

    iv. 1959. pp.100. [1811.]

    v. 1960. pp.108. [1920.]

    vi. 1961. pp.104. [1744.]

in progress.

EVIDENČNÝ súpis plánovaných bibliografických prác na Slovensku. Matica slovenská: Martin.*

    i. 1956.

    ii. 1957.

    iii. 1958.

    iv. 1959.

    v. 1960.

    vi. 1961. pp.200. [365.]

[KURT FLEISCHHACK, *ed.*], Bibliographie der versteckten bibliographien aus deutschsprachigen büchern und zeitschriften der jahre 1930–1953. Bearbeitet von der Deutschen bücherei. Deutsche bücherei: Sonderbibliographien (no.3): Leipzig 1956. pp.371. [10,000.]

— [supplement]. Bibliographie der deutschen bibliographien. Jahresverzeichnis der selbständig erschienenen und der in deutschsprachigen büchern und zeitschriften versteckten bibliographien. Bearbeitet von der Deutschen bücherei. Leipzig.

    i. 1954. 1957. pp.140. [3000.]

    ii. 1955. 1958. pp.219. [5500.]

    iii. 1956. 1959. pp.227. [5500.]

    iv. 1957. 1960. pp.252. [6000.]

    v–vi. 1958–1959. 1962. pp.515. [10,000.]

    vii. 1960. 1963. pp.388. [7000.]

in progress.

CURT FLEISCHHACK, ERNST RÜCKERT and GÜNTHER REICHARDT, Grundriss der bibliographie. Lehrbücher für den nachwuchs an wissenschaftlichen bibliotheken (vol.ii): Leipzig 1957. pp.viii. 263. [1500.]

SELECTIVE check lists of bibliographical scholarship 1949–1955. University of Virginia: Bibliographical society: Charlottesville 1957. pp.viii. 192. [3416.]

JÓZEF KORPALA, Abriss der geschichte der bibliographie in Polen. Staatssekretariat für hochschulwesen: Bibliothekskommission für publikationen und ausbildungsfragen: Bibliothekswissenschaftliche arbeiten aus der Sowjetunion und den ländern der volksdemokratie in deutscher übersetzung (ser.B, vol.ii): Leipzig 1957. pp.258. [1000.]

J[ULIETTE] [L.] DARGENT, Quelques bibliographies internationales, 1945–1956. Commission belge de bibliographie: Bibliographia belgica (no.28): Bruxelles 1957. pp.[ii].59. [475.]*

G. LORPHÈVRE, Les publications bibliographiques et de documentation éditées par l'Unesco. Commission belge de bibliographie: Bibliographia belgica (no.27): Bruxelles 1957. pp.[28]. [179.]*

BIBLIOGRAPHISCHE beihefte der Zeitschrift für bibliothekswesen und bibliographie. Frankfurt am Main.

> 1957. Herausgegeben von E[rich] Zimmermann. pp.98. [1554.]
> 1958. pp.118. [1532.]
> [*continued as:*]

Bibliographische berichte. Im auftrag des Deutschen bibliographischen kuratoriums bearbeitet.

> i. 1959. pp.[vi].131. [1618.]
> ii. 1960. pp.[v].91. [1458.]

iii. 1961. pp.[vii].149. [1890.]
in progress.

БИБЛИОТЕЧНО-БИБЛИОГРАФИЧЕСКИЙ бюлле-
тень. Выпуск 1. Академия наук Казахской
ССР: Центральная научная библиотека:
Алма-Ата 1958. pp.187. [1500.]

I[RAIDA] K[ONSTANTINOVNA] KIRPICHEVA, Библиография в помощь научной работе.
Методическое и справочное пособие. Государственная ... библиотека имени М. Е.
Салтыкова-Щедрина: Ленинград 1958. pp.
480. [1000.]
— — Handbuch der russischen und sowjetischen bibliographien. [Translated by Regina
Stein]. Bibliothekwissenschaftliche arbeiten aus
der Sowjetunion und den ländern der volksdemokratie in deutscher übersetzung (ser. B, vol.5):
Leipzig 1962. pp.228. [569.]

[G. B. KOLTUIPINA, E. P. KORSHUNOVA and A. D.
RKLITSKAYA],. Справочно-библиографическая
работа областной библиотеки. Методическое
пособие. Государственная ... Библиотека
СССР имени В. И. Ленина: Научно-методический кабинет библиотековедения. Отдел

справочно - библиографической и информационной работы: Москва 1958. pp.144. [200.]

БИБЛИОТЕКОВЕДЕНИЕ и библиография. 1958 &c.

details of this work are entered under Libraries, below.

LEOPOLDINA NAGY, A Szegedi egyetemi könyvtar külföldi bibliográfiái. A Szegedi egyetemi könyvtár kiadványai (no.43): Szeged 1959. pp.xi. 106. [777].*

KNUD LARSEN, Fortegnelse over bibliografier (foreløbig udgave). Danmarks biblioteksskole: København 1959. ff.[ii].73. [700.]*

LEOPOLDÍNA NAGY, A Szegedi egyetemi könyvtár kälföldi bibliográfiái. A Szegedi egyetemi könyvtár kiadványai (no.43): Szeged 1959.

[ANNEMARIE MEINER], Grundstock einer fachbibliothek für den buchhändler. [2. . . . auflage]. Frankfurt am Main [1959]. pp.54. [250.]

БИБЛИОТЕКОВЕДЕНИЕ и библиография. Указатель литературы. Государственная... библиотека СССР имени В. И. Ленина [&c.]: Москва.

 1959. [By G. S. Multanovskaya *and others*].

pp.135+132+123+120. [2561.]
1960. pp.129+116+112+120. [2745.]
1961. pp.144+108+104+136. [2938.]
in progress.

YU[RY] I[VANOVICH] MASANOV, Теория и практика библиографии. Указатель литературы 1917–1958. Всесоюзная книжная палата: Москва 1960. pp.480. [5477.]

F. G. WAGNER, Bibliotheca bibliographica librorum sedecimi saeculi. Bibliotheca bibliographica aureliana (vol.iii): Aureliae Aquensis 1960. pp.98. [2133.]

[LAURA MAIA DE FIGUEIREDO, *ed.*], Bibliografia brasileira de documentação. Instituto brasileiro de bibliografia e documentação: Rio de Janeiro [1960]. pp.237. [1129.]

BIBLIOGRAPHIES in the ECAFE library. United nations: [Economic commission for Asia and the far east:] Library: Bibliographical bulletin (no.1): Bangkok 1960. pp.[iv].34. [300.]*

A MAGYAR bibliográfiák bibliográfiája. Országos Széchényi könyvtár: Budapest.
1956–1957. Összeállította Bélley Pál és Ferenczyné Wendelin Lidia. 1960. pp.224. [913.]

34

1958–1960. Összeállította Ferenczyné Wendelin Lidia, Fügedi Péterné és Somogyi Andrásné. 1963. pp.420. [2191.]
in progress.

KNUD [ANDREAS] LARSEN, Fortegnelse over bibliografier. Danmarks biblioteksskole: København 1961. pp.117. [400.]*

I. V. GUDOVSHCHIKOVA, Библиография в Соединенных Штатах Америки. Ленинградский . . . институт им. Н. К. Крупской: Ленинград 1961. pp.88. [100.]

GÖSTA OTTERVIK, Bibliografier. Kommenterad urvalsförteckning med särskild hänsyn till svenska förhållanden. Sveriges allmänna biblioteksförening: Handböcker (no.13): Lund 1962. pp.xxiv. 169. [1500.]

B[ORIS] L[VOVICH] KANDEL, Библиография русских библиографий по зарубежной художественной литературе и литературоведению. Государственная . . . публичная библиотека имени М. Е. Салтыкова–Щедрина: Ленинград 1962. pp.180. [772.]

G[RIGORY] G[RIGOREVICH] KRICHEVSKY, Общие библиографии зарубежных стран. Ака-

демия наук СССР: Фундаментальная библиотека общественных наук: Москва 1962.
pp.290. [450.]

HENRIK GRÖNROOS, Finlands bibliografiska litteratur till 1962. Svenska medborgarhögskol: Hel-
singfors 1962. ff.59. [370.]*

BIBLIOGRAPHY in Britain. A classified list of
books and articles published in the United King-
dom. Oxford bibliographical society: Oxford.*
    i. 1962. [Edited by John Simon Gabriel
      Simmons]. pp.xiv.38. [408.]
in progress.

B. WYNAR, Introduction to bibliography and
reference books. A guide materials and bibliographical sources. University of Denver: Graduate school of librarianship: Denver 1963. pp.
viii.228.

L[IDIYA] I[VANOVNA] ZBRALEVICH and S[VET-
LANA] V[LADIMIROVNA] FEDULOVA, Библиография белорусской советской библиографии
1922–1961. Указатель. Академия наук Белорусской ССР: Минск 1963. pp.268. [1935.]

TODOR BOROV [*and others*], Die bibliographie in
den europäischen ländern der volksdemokratie.

Bibliography

Bibliothekswissenschaftliche arbeiten aus der Sowjetunion und den ländern der volksdemokratie in deutscher übersetzung (ser. B, vol.iii): Leipzig 1960. pp.165. [500.]

AKHTAR H. SIDDIQUI, Bibliography of bibliographies published in Pakistan. Pakistan bibliographical working group: Publication (no.4): Karachi 1961. pp.[ii].8. [50.]

DOCUMENTATION. An ASTIA report bibliography. Armed services technical information agency: Arlington, Va. 1961. [1962]. pp.v.278. [750.]*

2. Periodicals

LIST of current specialized abstracting and indexing services. International federation for documentation: Publication (no.235): The Hague 1949. pp.23. [1500.]*

D. H. BORCHARDT, Union list of periodicals on library science and bibliography held in the major libraries of Australia. University of Tasmania: Hobart 1953. pp.iv.25. [150.]*

ABSTRACTING and indexing journals. South african council for scientific and industrial research:

Library and information division: Pretoria 1955.
pp.vi.71. [199.]*

W. VAN DER BRUGGHEN, Library and documentation periodicals. Preliminary edition. International
federation for documentation: FID publ[ication]
(no.295): The Hague 1956. pp.36. [350.]
— — Second . . . edition. . . . (no.336): 1961.
pp.30. [500.]

SIIKA TANCHEVA, Чуждестранни текущи
библиографии, получавани в българския
библиографски институт. Анотиран списък.
Български библиографски институт: Поредица периодичен печат (no.8): София 1956.
pp.56. [171.]

FR[ANÇOIS] JOANNAUX, Revues bibliographiques internationales et revues belges. Commission
belge de bibliographie: Bibliographia belgica
(no.38): Bruxelles 1958. pp.[iii].xvi.364. [1664.]*
*the title is misleading: lists periodicals containing
bibliographies.*

L[OUISE] N[OËLLE] MALCLÈS, Rapport sur les
bibliographies internationales spécialisées courantes en France. Commission nationale de bibliographie: 1953. pp.113. [234.]*

——[another edition]. Les bibliographies internationales spécialisées courantes françaises ou à participation française. [By Andrée Lhéritier]. Direction des bibliothèques de France: Commission nationale de bibliographie: Paris 1958. pp.96. [253.]

NÓMINA de publicaciones periódicas de bibliotecología y documentación existentes en la biblioteca. Universidad: Instituto bibliotecológico: Buenos Aires 1958. ff.[i].ii.20. [101.]*

R. G. GITMAN [*and others*], Иностранные периодические издания по библиографии и библиотековедению, имеющиеся в библиотеках Москвы и Ленинграда. Сводный каталог. Всесоюзная государственная библиотека иностранной литературы: Москва 1959. pp.171. [2000.]

[CLARA LOUISE KUEHN and WINIFRED F. DESMOND], A guide to the world's abstracting and indexing services in science and technology. National federation of science abstracting and indexing services: Report (no.102): Washington 1963. pp.viii.183. [1855.]

VERZEICHNIS laufend erscheinender bibliographien. Deutsche forschungsgemeinschaft: Wiesbaden 1963. pp.90. [727.]

РЕФЕРАТИВНЫЙ журнал и экспресс-информация. Moscow 1964. pp.174. [350.]

3. *Bibliographies of national bibliographies*

ROBERT ALEXANDER PEDDIE, National bibliographies: a descriptive catalogue of the works which register the books published in each country. 1912. pp.vi.34. [150.]

JORIS VORSTIUS, Der gegenwärtige stand der primären nationalbibliographie in den kulturländern. Leipzig 1930. pp.38. [35.]

OLGA PINTO, Repertori bibliografici nazionali. Firenze 1931. pp.58. [300.]

OLGA PINTO, Le bibliografie nazionali. Enciclopedia del libro: Milano 1935. pp.5–117. [400.]
— — Secunda edizione. Biblioteca di bibliografia italiana (vol.xx): Firenze 1951. pp.94. [400.]
a supplement by the author appears in La Bibliofilia (*Firenze 1957*), *lix.35–54.*

LAWRENCE HEYL, Current national bibliographies. A list of sources of information concerning current books of all countries. . . . Revised edition. American library association: Chicago 1942. ff.[ii].19. [125.]*

HELEN F[IELD] CONOVER, Current national bibliographies. Library of Congress: General reference and bibliography division: Washington 1955. pp.v.132. [249.]★

MÁRIA L. ČERNÁ, Národné bibliografie. Príručka pre poslucháčov knihovedy a pre knihovníkov. Matica slovenská: Príručky pre knihovníkov (no.9): Martin 1955. pp.[iii].308. [1250.]★

RUDOLF BLUM, Vor- und frühgeschichte der nationalen allgemeinbibliographie. Archiv für geschichte des buchwesens: [Frankfurt am Main 1959]. pp.233–303. [200.]

I. V. GUDOVSHCHIKOVA, Библиография в европейских странах народной демократии. Учебное пособие для студентов по курсу "общая иностранная библиография". Ленинградский государственный библиотечный институт имени Н. К. Крупской: Ленинград 1960. pp.92. [20.]

G[RIGORY] G[RIGOREVICH] KRICHEVSKY, Общие библиографии зарубежных стран. Академия наук СССР: Фундаментальная библиотека общественных наук: Москва 1962. pp.292. [541.]

K[ONSTANTIN] R[OMANOVICH] SIMON, История иностранной библиографии. Академия наук СССР : Фундаментальная библиотека общественных наук: Москва 1963. pp.736. [3000.]

4. *Bibliographies of personal bibliographies*

[N. YOUNG], A list of bibliographies of authors (literary and scientific). 1932. pp.[ii].ff.9. [275.]
200 copies printed.

MAX ARNIM, Internationale personalbibliographie, 1850–1935. Leipzig 1936. pp.iii–xii.572. [30,000.]

— — Internationale personalbibliographie, 1800–1943. . . . Zweite . . . auflage. 1944–1952. pp.xvi.706+[iii].834. [75,000.]

— — Fortgeführt von Gerhard Bock und Franz Hodes. Band III. 1944–1959, und nachträge zur 2. auflage von band I–II. 1961–
in progress.

5. *Universal bibliographies*

CONRAD GESNER, Bibliotheca vniuersalis, siue catalogus omnium scriptorum locupletissimus, in tribus linguis, latina, græca, & hebraica: extantium & non extentiū, ueterum & recentiorum in hunc usꝗ diem, doctorum & indoctorum publicatorum & in bibliothecis latentium. Opus nouum, &: nō bibliothecis tantum publicis priuatísue instituendis necessarium, sed studiosis omnibus instituendis necessarium, sed studiosis omnibus cuiuscunqʒ artis aut scientiæ ad studia melius formanda utilissimum. Tigvri 1545. ff.[xviii].631. [15,000.]

—— Appendix. 1555. ff.[viii].106. [4000.]

—— [Secvndvs . . . tomus]. Pandectarvm sive partitionum uniuersalium Conradi Gesneri Tigurini, medici & philosophiæ professoris, libri xxi. Tigvri 1548. ff.[vi].375. [37,500.]

actually contains only the first nineteen books; the twentieth (medicine) was not published, while the twenty-first was issued separately, thus:

—— — Partitiones theologicæ, pandectarum vniuersalium Conradi Gesneri liber ultimus. . . . Accedit index alphabeticus præsenti libro & superioribus xix. communis. Tiguri 1549. ff.[viii].157. [xiii]. [15,000.]

—— Elenchvs scriptorvm omnivm . . . ante annos aliquot à . . . Conrado Gesnero . . . editus, nūc ueró primùm in reipublicæ literariæ gratiam in compendium redactus, & autorum haud pœnitenda accessione auctus: per Conradvm Lycosthenem. Basilæ 1551. pp.[xvi].coll.1096.pp.[xxiii]. [10,000.]

—— Epitome Bibliothecae Conradi Gesneri, conscripta primum à Conrado Lycosthene Rubeaquensi nunc denuo recognita & locupletata: per Iosiam Simlerum Tigvrinvm. Tiguri 1555. ff. [vi].184.[xiii]. [20,000.]

— — Bibliotheca institvta et collecta primvm a Conrado Gesnero, deinde in epitomen redacta & nouorum librorū accessione locupletata, iam vero postremo recognita,&indup lum post priores editiones aucta, per Iosiam Simlerum. Tigvri 1574. pp.[x].691.[xl]. [35,000.]

— — Bibliotheca institvta et collecta primvm a Conrado Gesnero, deinde in epitomen redacta. ... Iam verò postremò aliquot mille, cùm priorum tùm nouorum authorum opusculis, ex instructissima Viennensi Austriæ Imperatoria bibliotheca amplificata, per Iohannen Iacobum Frisium. Tigvri 1583. pp.[lvi].838. [45,000.]

— — Svpplementvm epitomes bibliothecæ Gesnerianæ. Quo longè plurimi continentur qui Conrad. Gesnerum, Ios. Simlerum & Io. Iac. Frisium postremum huiusce bibliothecæ locupletatorum latuerunt, vel post eorum editiones typis mandati sunt Antonio Veŕderio domino Vallipriuatæ collectore. Lvgdvni 1585. pp.70. [2000.]

the date is misprinted CIƆ. IƆ. IƆXXCV on the title-page; published as a supplement to Du Verdier's Bibliothèque; *see also in the next section, under Robert Constantin, 1555.*

Bibliography

JOHANN CLESS, Vnivs secvli, eivsqve virorvm literatorvm monvmentis tvm florentissimi, tvm fertilissimi: ab anno Dom. 1500. ad. 1602. nundinarum autumnalium inclusiue, elenchus consummatissimus librorvm hebræi, græci, latini, germani, aliorumque Europæ jdiomatum: typorum æternitati consecratorum. . . . Desvmptvs partim ex singvlarvm nundinarum catalogis, partim ex instructissimis vbq; locorum bibliothecis. Francofvrti 1602. pp.[x].563+[vii].292. [15,000.]

the title of the second part reads Catalogi librorvm germanicorvm alphabetici . . . secvnda pars.

FABIANUS JUSTINIANUS, Index vniversalis alphabeticvs materias in omni facultate consulto pertractatas, earumq. scriptores, & locos designans, appendice perampla locupletatus. Elenchvs item avctorvm qvi in sacra Biblia vel vniuersè, vel singulatim, etiam in versiculos, data opera, scripserunt. Romae 1612. pp.[viii].648.95. [60,000.]

reissued with a cancelled p.223 and a different preface; the four Bibliothèque nationale copies present all the variations.

[GEORG DRAUD], Bibliotheca exotica, siue catalogvs, officinalis librorvm peregrinis lingvis, vsvalibvs scriptorvm, videlicet gallica, italica, hispanica, belgica, anglica, danica, bohemica, vngarica &c. Frankfovrt 1625. p.302. [6000.]

Bibliography

GEORG MATTHIAS KÖNIG, Bibliotheca vetus et nova, in qua hebræorum, chaldæorum, syrorum, arabum, persarum, ægyptiorum, græcorum & latinorum per universum terrarum orbem scriptorum . . . patria, ætas, nomina, libri . . . à prima mundi origine ad annum asqʒ M.DC.LXXIX . . . recensentur. Altdorfi 1678. pp.[xii].888. [35,000.]

MARTINUS LIPENIUS, Bibliotheca realis universalis omnium materiarum, rerum et titulorum, in theologia, jurisprudentia, medicina et philosophia occurrentium. Francofurti ad Moenum [1679–] 1685. pp.[clxxviii].748 + [ii].944.[iv] + [xii].560. [li] + [xix].492.[42] + [viii].864 + [ii].865–1594. [106]. [125,000.]

CHRISTOPH HENDREICH, Pandectæ brandenburgicæ, continentes I. Bibliothecam, seu magnam, &, si additamenta accesserint, maximam auctorum impressorum & manuscr. partem: quibus adduntur auctorum quorundam vitæ, delectus; nomina plurimorum anonymorum, pseudonymorum &c. explicata. Idque in omnibus fere scientiis, & orbis terrarum linguis, II. Indicem materiarum præcipuarum, in iis contentarum: utrumque ordin. alphabetico. Berolini 1699. pp.[iii].816. [50,000.]

A–B of part 1 only; no more published.

46

[JOHANN BURKHARDT MENCKEN], Compendiöses gelehrten-lexicon, darinnen die gelehrten . . . welche vom anfang der welt, . . . sich durch schrifften oder sonst der gelehrten welt bekant gemacht, . . . beschrieben werden. Leipzig 1715. pp.[xvi].coll.2682.[vi]. [30,000.]

— — Henrici Johannis Bytemeister . . . Specimen supplementorum et emendationum lexici . . . cujus inscriptio: Compendioses gelehrten-lexicon . . . ut vulgo loquuntur. [Helmstadii 1726]. pp.24. [400.]

— — Die andere auflage . . . vermehret durch m. Christian Gottlieb Jöcher. 1726. pp.[xxviii]. coll.1628+pp.[ii].coll.1682.[vi]. [40,000.]

— — Die dritte auflage, herausgegeben von C. G. Jöcher. 1733. pp.[xxviii].coll.1888+2102. [viii]. [50,000.]

ALFONSUS CIACONIUS [ALONSO CHACON] Bibliotheca libros et scriptores ferme cunctos ab initio mundi ad annum MDLXXXIII. ordine alphabetico complectens. . . . Nunc primum in lucem prodit studio & cum observationibus Francisci Dionysii Camusati. Parisiis 1731. pp.[iv].xxviii.coll.976. pp.[iii]. [20,000.]

A–Epimenides only; no more published.

— — [another edition]. Bibliotheca. . . . Primum in lucem prolata Parisiis MDCCXXIX [sic]. . . . Acces-

serunt nunc ejusdem de Germanis quibusdam . . .
& de scriptoribus elogiorum ac vitarum virorum
illustrium judicia . . . opera Joannis Erhardi Kappii.
Amstelodami &c. 1744. pp.[iv].lxii.coll.996.pp.
[ii]. [22,500.]

MICHAEL A. S. JOSEPH. Bibliographia critica,
sacra et prophana. Matriti 1740–1742. pp.[lvi].548
+[ii].575+[vii].600+[xviii].508. [25,000.]
— — Admonitiones in volumina I, II et III.
Bibliographiæ criticæ . . . exhibitæ a . . . Hyacintho
Segura. Valentiæ 1742. pp.xx.205.[iii].viii. [50.]

THEOPHIL GEORGI, Allgemeines europäisches bü-
cher-lexicon. Leipzig 1742–1753. pp.[iv.]398+
458+238[*sic*, 328]+350+[iii].404. [100,000.]
— — Svpplement. 1750. pp.[ii].400. [20,000.]
— —́ Zweytes svpplement. 1755. pp.[ii].390.
[20,000.]
— — Drittes svpplement. 1758. pp.[iv].408.
[20,000.]

ABRAHAM FERWERDA, Catalogus universalis cum
pretiis . . . in eene alphabetische order geschikt,
met de pryzen hoe veel elke boek in ieder ver-
kopinge gekost heeft. Leeuwarden [*c*.1772–1779].
  [A]. 1ste deel, 1ste stuk: behelzende de latyn-
    sche boeken in folio. [*c*.1772]. pp.[xiv].476.
    [iv]. [3250.]

— — Register van alle rare en zeldzaam voorkomende latynsche boeken in folio, . . . gedrukt in het jaar 1400, of in de xvde eeuw. [*c.*1774]. pp.175. [1400.]

— — Supplementum. [*c.*1773]. pp.[viii].464 +328. [7000.]

— 2de [–4de] stuk: behelzende de latynsche boeken in quarto. [*c.*1772–1773]. pp.422+ 426+509. [10,000.]

— 5de [–13de] stuk: behelzende de latynsche boeken in octavo, &c. [*c.*1777–1779]. pp.[i]. 244 + [i].355 + [i].320 + [i].310 + [i].344 + [i].384 + [i].455 + [i].336 + [i].127. [22,500.]

[B]. Allgemeene naam-lyst van boeken met de pryzen. 1ste deel, 1ste stuk: behelzende de nederduitsche boeken in folio en quarto. [*c.*1772]. pp.[vii].365.[iii]. [2500.]

— 2de [–3de] stuk: behelzende de nederduitsche boeken in octavo. [*c.*1772–1773]. pp. [i].301+270.[ix]. [4500.]

  includes a very short appendix of incunabula.

[C]. Catalogue universelle [*sic*] avec les prix. 1ste deel, 1ste stuk: behelzende de fransche boeken in folio. [*c.*1772]. pp.[viii].206. [1400.]

— 2de stuk: behelzende de fransche boeken

in quarto. [*c*.1773]. pp.308. [2250.]

— 3de [–4de] stuk: behelzende de fransch boeken in octavo. [*c*.1773–1774]. pp.[i].336 +335. [5500.]

this work consolidates the catalogues of about 300 book auctions between 1702 and 1778; it is from these dates, as shown in the text, that the suggested dates of publication are inferred; except as shown above incunabula are not included, and it is therefore possible that a Register *was published for each section.*

ROBERT WATT, Bibliotheca britannica; or a general index to british and foreign literature. Edinburgh 1824. pp.[ii].vii.807+[694]+[694]+[836]. [150,000.]

JOHANN GEORG THEODOR GRÄSSE, Lehrbuch einer allgemeinen literärgeschichte aller bekannten völker der welt, von der ältesten bis auf die neuere [neueste] zeit. Dresden &c. [*afterwards:* Leipzig].

    i. Lehrbuch einer literärgeschichte der berühmtesten völker der alten welt, oder geschichte der literatur der Aegypter, Assyrer, Juden, Armenier, Chinesen, Perser, Inder, Griechen und Römer, vom anfange der literärischen kultur bis zum untergange des Weströmischen reiches. 1837–1838. pp. xii.516+[v].517–1350. [25,000.]

ii. Lehrbuch einer literärgeschichte der berühmtesten völker des mittelalters, oder geschichte der literatur der Araber, Armenier, Perser, Türken, Syrer, Juden, Chinesen, Inder, Griechen, Italiäner, Engländer, Franzosen, Deutschen, Spanier, Portugiesen, Slaven und der völker der Scandinavischen halbinsel vom untergange des Weströmischen reiches bis zur zerstörung des Oströmischen kaiserthums. 1839–1843. pp. xii.874 + [v].1242 + xviii.492 + iv.493–1350. [60,000.]

iii. 1. Das sechszehnte jahrhundert in seinen schriftstellern und ihren werken auf den verschiedenen gebieten der wissenschaften und schönen künste. 1852. pp.x.1284. [25,000.]

iii. 11. Das siebzehnte jahrhundert in seinen schriftstellern [&c.]. 1853. pp.[iii].1012. [20,000.]

iii. 111. Das achtzehnte und die erste hälfte des neunzehnten jahrhunderts in ihren schriftstellern [&c.]. 1858. pp.[viii].808+[iii].809–2008. [40,000.]

iv. Die sämmtlichen register enthaltend. 1859. pp.v.386.

— — Handbuch der allgemeinen literaturgeschichte. . . . Ein auszug aus des verfassers grösserem Lehrbuche. 1845–1850. pp.xvi.448+x.710+xii.1092+viii.1296.130. [40,000.]

WUTTIG's universal-bibliographie. . . . Verantwortlicher redacteur.... G. [W.] Wuttig. Leipzig 1862. pp.46. [2000.]
also issued with english and french titlepages; planned as a periodical, but no more published.

[LOUIS] G[USTAVE] VAPEREAU, Dictionnaire universel des littératures, contenant . . . des notices sur les écrivains de tous les temps et de tous les pays . . . la bibliographie générale et particulière, les ouvrages à consulter sur les questions d'histoire, de théorie et d'érudition. 1876[–1877]. pp.xvi.2096. [100,000.]

6. *Select universal bibliographies*

R[OBERT] CONSTANTIN, Nomenclator insignivm scriptorvm, qvorvm libri extant vel manuscripti, vel impressi: ex bibliothecis Galliæ, & Angliæ: indexque totius Bibliothecæ, atq; Pandectarū doctissimi atq; ingeniosissimi viri C. Gesneri. Parisiis 1555. p.189[iii]. [2000.]

[NICOLAUS BASSE], Collectio in vnvm corpvs,

omnivm librorvm hebræorum, græcorvm, latino-
rvm necnon germanicè, italicè, gallicè, & hispanicè
scriptorum, qui in nundinis francofurtensibus ab
anno 1564. vsque ad nundinas autumnales anni
1592. partim noui, partim noua forma, & diuersis
in locis editi, venales extiterunt: desumpta ex
omnibus catalogis VVillerianis singularum nundinarum. Francofvrti 1592. pp.[xvi].636+373+
[xvi].62. [15,000.]

ANTONIO POSSEVINO, Bibliotheca selecta, qua
agitur de ratione stvdiorvm in disciplinis, in salute
omnium procuranda. Romæ 1593. pp.[viii].664+
[viii].321+28.[xxiv]. [5000.]

ISRAEL SPACH, Nomenclatur scriptorvm philo-
sophicorvm atqve philologicorvm. Hoc est: svc-
cincta recensio eorvm, qvi philosophiam omnes-
qve eivs partes qvouis tempore idiomateúe [sic]
vsq; ad annum 1597 descripserunt, illustrarunt, &
exornarunt, methodo artificiosa secundum locos
communes ipsius philosophiæ. Argentinæ 1598.
pp.[xx].727.[c]. [10,000.]

the scope of this work is much wider than is sug-
gested by the title.

HENNING GROSS, Elenchus seu index generalis, in
quo continentur libri omnes, qui ultimo, seculi

1500. lustro, post annum 1593, usq; ad annum 1600. in S. Romano imperio & vicinis regionibus novi auctivè prodiêrunt. [Leipzig 1600]. pp.[364]. [4000.]

limited to latin books; the second part is entered under German literature: sixteenth century, below.

— — Continuatio tertia. 1660. pp.60. [600.]

PAULUS BOLDUANUS, Bibliotheca philosophica, sive: elenchus scriptorum philosophicorum atqve philologicorum illustrium. Jenæ 1616. pp.[xxiv]. 647.[viii]. [9000.]

the scope of this work is much wider than is suggested by the title.

FRANCISCUS DE ARAOZ, De bene disponenda bibliotheca, ad meliorem cognitionem loci & materiæ, qualitatisque librorum, litteratis perutile opvscvlvm. Matriti 1631. ff.[xxiv].57.[xi]. [250.]

JOHANN ANDREAS QUENSTEDT, Dialogus de patriis illustrium doctrina et scriptis virorum, omnium ordinum ac facultatum, qui ab initio mundi per universum terrarum orbem usq; ad annum . . . M.DC. claruerunt. Wittebergæ 1654. pp.[xxiv]. 692.[lxx]. [4000.]

— — [Another edition]. 1691.

Bibliography

EDWARD LEIGH, A treatise of religion & learning, and of religious and learned men. 1656. pp. [x].373.[xxxiv]. [5000.]

SIMON PAULLI, Historia literaria, sive dispositio librorum omnium facultatum ac artium secundum materias. Argentorati 1671. pp.[xvi].182.[liii]. [4000.]

a continuation of this work is entered under Italian literature: Select, below.

[JOHANN HEINRICH BOECLER], Bibliographia historico-politico-philologica curiosa, quid in quovis scriptore laudem censuramve mereatur, exhibens. [Edited by Samuel Schottelius]. Germanopoli 1677. pp.[348]. [2000.]

[—] — [another edition]. 1696. pp.[365]. [2000.]
— — [another edition]. Bibliographia critica scriptores omnivm artvm atqve scientiarvm ordine percensens, nvnc demvm integra et emendativs edita accessionibvsque ex reliqvis scriptis Boeclerianis avcta, recensvit Io[hann] Gottlieb Kravse. Lipsiæ 1715. pp.[lxiv].904.[lxii]. [5000.]

CATALOGUS cujuscunque facultatis & linguæ librorum abhinc 2 a 3 annorum spatio in Germania, Gallia, & Belgio, &c. novissime impressorum. Singulis semestribus continuandus. Amstelædami 1678. pp.[iii].35. [750.]

iii. July 1676–January 1677. pp.40. [750.]
iv. January–July 1677. pp.[ii].36. [500.]
v. July 1677–January 1678. pp.[ii].27. [250.]
vi. January–July 1678. pp.[iv].40. [400.]
vii. July 1678–January 1679. pp.[ii].30. [250.]
viii. January–July 1679. pp.[ii].49. [500.]
ix. July 1679–January 1680. pp.[iii].52. [500.]
x. January–July 1680. pp.[ii].49. [250.]
xi. July 1680–January 1681. pp.[ii].35. [250.]
xii. January–July 1681. pp.[ii].28. [200.]
xiii. July 1681–January 1682. pp.[ii].26. [200.]
xiv. January–July 1682. pp.[ii].37. [250.]
xv. July 1682–January 1683. pp.[ii].32. [250.]
xvi. January–July 1683. pp.[ii].29. [200.]
xvii. July 1683–January 1684. pp.[ii].58. [300.]

*the first issue also contains the first two semesters;
the title varies slightly, the scope of the work not being
limited to the countries first named.*

JOHANN GEORG SCHIELEN, Bibliotheca enucleata.
Sev artifodina artium ac scientiarum omnium.
Exhibens apographa, elenchos, et pericopas in
jurisprudentia, physica, medicina, politica, mathe-
matica, et philosophia, nec non in sacris ac propha-
nis historiis passim occurrentes. Ulmæ 1679. pp.
[xvi].624. [30,000.]

ACTA eruditorum anno M DC LXXXII [&c.]
publicata. Lipsiæ.

1682. [Edited by Otto Mencke]. pp.[x].402.
  [vi]. [175.]
1683. pp.[viii].561.[vii]. [225.]
1684. pp.[ix].591.[vii]. [200.]
1685. pp.[vi].595.[xii]. [325.]
1686. pp.[vi].3–630.[xi]. [250.]
1687. pp.[viii].704.[ix]. [200.]
1688. pp.[viii].672.[viii]. [175.]
1689. pp.[viii].653.[ix]. [200.]
1690. pp.[viii].611.[v]. [150.]
1691. pp.[viii].590.[vi]. [200.]
1692. pp.[ii].570.[xxviii]. [200.]
1693. pp.[ii].546.[xvi]. [200.]
1694. pp.[ii].518.[200.]
1695. pp.[ii].560.[lii]. [175.]
1696. pp.[ii].604. [175.]
1697. pp.[viii].594. [150.]
1698. pp.[ii].597. [175.]
1699. pp.[ii].582. [150.]
1700. pp.[ii].586. [175.]
1701. pp.[ii].582. [175.]
1702. pp.[ii].566. [175.]
1703. pp.[ii].582. [150.]
1704. pp.[ii].592. [175.]
1705. pp.[ii].590. [200.]
1706. pp.[ii].590. [200.]
1707. [Edited by Johann Burckhard Mencke].

pp.[ii].606. [200.]
1708. pp.[ii].559.[xxxix]. [175.]
1709. pp.[ii].547.[xliii]. [200.]
1710. pp.[iv].535.[xxxvii]. [200.]
1711. pp.[ii].560.[xxx], [200.]
1712. pp.[ii].555.[xxxv]. [200.]
1713. pp.[iv].559.[xxii]. [175.]
1714. pp.[ii].565.[xli]. [175.]
1715. pp.[ii].549.[xli]. [175.]
1716. pp.[ii].567.[xxxiii]. [175.]
1717. pp.[iv].553.[xxxix]. [200.]
1718. pp.[ii].564.[xxxix]. [200.]
1719. pp.[vi].540.[xxxviii]. [175.]
1720. pp.[ii].540.[xlviii]. [175.]
1721. pp.[iv].547.[xliv]. [175.]
1722. pp.[ii].571.[xxxv]. [150.]
1723. pp.[ii].543. [lv]. [175.]
1724. pp.[ii].543.[xlv]. [175.]
1725. pp.[ii].545.[xxxvii]. [175.]
1726. pp.[ii].543.[xxxvi]. [200.]
1727. pp.[iv].552.[xxxvi]. [175.]
1728. pp.[ii].562.[xxxii]. [200.]
1729. pp.[iv].552.[xxviii]. [225.]
1730. pp.[ii].561.[xxxvii]. [225.]
1731. pp.[iv].560.[xxxvi]. [225.]
[*continued as:*]
Nova acta eruditorum [&c.].

1732. [Edited by Friedrich Otto Mencke].
pp.[vi].594.[xxxii]. [200.]

1733. pp.[x].560.[xxx]. [125.]

1734. pp.[iv].608. [150.]

1735. pp.[iv].562.[xxxiv]. [150.]

1736. pp.[iv].562.[xxxiv]. [150.]

1737. pp.[iv].555.[xxxi]. [125.]

1738. pp.[vi].710.[xlii]. [175.]

1739. pp.[iv].720.[xliii]. [150.]

1740. pp.[vi].718.[xlii]. [150.]

1741. pp.[vi].720.[xlii]. [175.]

1742. pp.[iv].720.[xxxv]. [150.]

1743. pp.[iv].720.[xxxvi]. [150.]

1744. pp.[iv].720.[xxxvi]. [175.]

1745. pp.[iv].720.[xxviii]. [175.]

1746. pp.[iv].720.[xxxvi]. [175.]

1747. pp.[iv].720.[xxiv]. [125.]

1748. pp.[iv].716.[xxiv]. [150.]

1749. pp.[iv].720.[xxvii]. [175.]

1750. pp.[vi].722.[xxxvi]. [125.]

1751. pp.[iv].720.[xxiv]. [125.]

1752. pp.[viii].720.[xxii]. [150.]

1753. pp.[vi].720.[xxvi]. [150.]

1754. pp.[viii].720.[xxvi]. [150.]

1755. pp.[iv].720.[xxiv]. [150.]

1756. pp.[iv].716.[xxii]. [125.]

1757. pp.[iv].730.[xxvii]. [125.]

59

1758. pp.[iv].720.[xxvii]. [150.]

1759. pp.[iv].720.[xxx]. [125.]

1760. pp.[iv].622[*sic*, 672].[xxxviii]. [125.]

1761. pp.[iv].600.[xxiii]. [100.]

1762. pp.[iv].600.[xix]. [100.]

1763. pp.[iv].616.[xvi]. [75.]

1764–1765. pp.[iv].480.[xviii]. [50.]

1766–1767. pp.[iv].482.[xv]. [50.]

1768. pp.[iv].576.[xviii]. [75.]

1769. pp.[iv].576.[xx]. [75.]

1770. pp.[iv].580.[xii]. [50.]

1771. pp.[iv].586.[xviii]. [75.]

1772. 1774. pp.[iv].576.[xx]. [100.]

1773. 1776. pp.[iv].574.[xx]. [75.]

1774. 1777. pp.[iv].576.[xv]. [50.]

1775. 1779. pp.[iv].600.[xix]. [75.]

1776. 1779. pp.[iv].590.[xxvi]. [75.]

no more published; F. O. Mencke died in 1754.

— Actorum eruditorum quæ Lipsiæ publicantur supplementa. Lipsiæ.

i. 1692. pp.[iv].639.[v]. [225.]

ii. 1696. pp.[ii].603. [200.]

iii. 1702. pp.[ii].565[*sic*, 574]. [150.]

iv. 1711. pp.[ii].531[*sic*, 534].[xxxvi]. [200.]

v. 1713. pp.[ii].541.[xxvii]. [175.]

vi. 1717. pp.[ii].543.[xxxi]. [175.]

vii. 1721. pp.[ii].537.[xlvii]. [150.]

viii. 1724. pp.[ii].532.[xxxiv]. [150.]
ix. 1729. pp.[ii].509.[xxiv]. [150.]
x. 1734. pp.[iv].560.[xxxv]. [200.]
    [continued as:]

Ad nova acta eruditorum, quæ Lipsiæ publicantur, supplementa.

i. 1735. pp.[viii].627.[xxix]. [200.]
ii. 1737. pp.[iv].552.[xxxv]. [200.]
iii. 1739. pp.[iv].552.[xxxi]. [200.]
iv. 1742. pp.[iv].552.[xxxii]. [175.]
v. 1745. pp.[iv].552.[xxxii]. [200.]
vi. 1749. pp.[iv].552.[xxviii]. [200.]
vii. 1754. pp.[iv].550.[xlii]. [175.]
viii. 1757. pp.[iv].544.[xx]. [100.]

—— Indices generales avctorvm et rervm
primi [&c.] Actorvm ervditorvm quæ Lipsiæ
publicantur decennii, nec non svpplementorvm
tomi primi [&c.].

[1682–1691; supp. i]. 1693. pp.[406].
[1692–1701; supp. ii–iii]. 1704. pp.[380].
[1702–1711; supp. iv–v]. 1714. pp.[496].
[1712–1721; supp. v–vii]. 1723. pp.[504].
[1722–1731; supp. viii–x]. 1733. pp.[540].
[1732–1741; supp. i–iv]. 1745. pp.[612].

[PAUL] COLOMIÈS, Bibliothèque choisie. La Rochelle 1682. pp.[iv].208. [100.]

— — Deuxième édition. Amsterdam 1700. pp. 216. [100.]

— — Nouvelle édition. Paris 1731. pp.xxii.376. xx.[100.]

this edition is found with the imprints of various publishers.

ANTOINE TEISSIER, Les éloges des hommes savans, tirez de l'Histoire de m. de Thou. Avec . . . le catalogue de leurs ouvrages. Genève 1683. pp. [xlv].600.[xxi]+432. [2500.]

— — Seconde édition. Utrecht 1696. pp.[xxiv]. 524+391.[xxxix]. [4000.]

reissued in 1697.

— — — Nouvelles additions. Berlin 1704. pp. [xxxv].464.[xv]. [250.]

also described as 'tome troisième'.

— — Quatrième édition, Leyde 1715. pp. [xxxvi].411.[v].20+474.[v]+462.[ii].+546.[xiv]. [5000.]

[ADRIEN BAILLET], Jugemens des sçavans sur les principaux ouvrages des auteurs. 1685–1686. pp. [xxxiii].616 + [ii].329.[lxiv] + 595 + [vi].702 + [iv].208.274 + [ii].568 + [ii].438 + [ii].215.324 + [ii].484. [5000.]

— — Revûs, corrigés, & augmentés par m. [Bernard] de la Monnoye. 1722. pp.[xx].xxviii.81.

405 + [vi].680.[xvi] + [ii].464.[iii] + [ii].488.[iii]
+ [ii].461.[ix] + [vi].238.[x].241–255. [ii] + [x].
388.[civ]+xxxii.635. [5000.]

part of the first volume, with ms. notes by Barthé-
lemy Mercier de Saint-Léger, is in the Bibliothèque
nationale.

—— Revûs, corrigéz, & augmentes par mr. de
la Monnoye. Nouvelle édition. Amsterdam 1725.
pp.[xii].xlvii.572.[iv] + [ii].159 + [x].429 + [ii].
406 + [ii].592 + [ii].455 + [ii].468 + [ii].573 +
[ii].627 + [x].424 + [ii].596 + [ii].xv.432 + [ii].
464 + xix.550 + [ii].562 + xliv.576. + [iv].640.
[5000.]

——— [another edition of the same text in
larger format]. Amsterdam 1725. pp.[vi].lxxvii.
237 + [vii].478 + [ii].310 + [ii].402 + [vi].350 +
[ii].vi.299+viii.379+xvi.408. [5000.]

TH[OMAS] BARTHOLINUS, De libris legendis dis-
sertationes VII . . editæ à Th. Bartholino filio.
Hafniæ 1686. pp.[xxxii].308. [500.]

—— Quas...publicæ luci restituit...Joh. Gerh.
Menschen. Francofurti 1711. pp.[xlvii].192. [500.]
this edition was also issued with a Hagae Comitum
imprint.

[GEORGE WELLS], The universal historical bib-
liotheque: or an account of most of the consider-

able books printed in all languages in the month of
January [February, March], 1686. Wherein a short
description is given of the design and scope of almost every book: and of the quality of the author,
if known. 1687. pp.[vi].67+[viii].69–131+[ii].
135–203. [70.]

PAUL FREHER, Theatrum virorum eruditione cla-
rorum, in quo vitae et scripta theologorum, jure-
consultorum, medicorum et philosophorum tam
in Germania ... quam in aliis Europae regionibus
... a seculis aliquot ad haec usque tempora floren-
tium. [Edited by Carl Joachim Freher]. Noribergae
1688. pp.vi.1562.[xv]. [20,000.]

DANIEL GEORG MORHOF, Polyhistor sive de notitia
auctorum et rerum commentarii, quibus praeterea
varia ad omnes disciplinas consilia et subsidia pro-
ponuntur. Lubecæ 1688–1692, pp.[viii].540 +
[xvi].160. [1000.]

—— Editio secunda.Lubecæ 1695. pp.[xx].556.
[1000.]

—— [another edition]. Accuratè revisum ... a
Johanne Möllero. Lubecæ 1708. pp.[xviii].768.406
+[ii].534.130.[ccviii]. [7500.]

—— Editio secvnda. Maximam partem opvs
posthvmvm, accuratè revisum, emendatum, ex
autoris annotationibus αὐτογράφοις, &mss.aliis,

suppletum passim atque auctum . . . à Johanne Möllero. Lvbecæ 1714. pp.[vi].80.1072+604. [ccviii]. [7500.]

—— Editio tertia. Cum accessionibus . . . Ioannis Frickii et Iohannis Molleri . . . Præfationem, notitiamque diariorum litterariorum Europæ præmisit Io. Albertus Fabricius. Lubecæ 1732. pp. [xlvi].1072+[ii].604.[ccviii]. [7500.]

—— Editio quarta. Cui præfationem . . . præmisit Io. Albertus Fabricius . . . nunc auctam ft [*sic*] ad annum MDCCXLVII. continuatam [by J. J. Schwabe]. Lubecæ 1747. pp.[liv].1072+[ii].604. [ccviii]. [7500.]

the texts of the 1714, 1732, 1747 editions are identical.

DANIEL HARTNACCIUS, Anweisender bibliothecarius der studierenden jugend, durch die vornehmsten wissenschaften. Stockholm &c. 1690. pp.[xxxii].112.352. [3000.]

[SIR] THOMAS POPE BLOUNT, Censura celebriorum authorum: sive tractatus in quo varia virorum doctorum de clarissimis cujusque seculi scriptoribus judicia traduntur. Londini 1690. pp.[vii].746. [vi]. [15,000.]

—— Editio nova. Genevae 1694. pp.vii.1070. [15,000.]

—— Editio nova correctior. 1710. pp.[vii]. 1063.[vii]. [15,000.]

[JOHN HARTLEY], Catalogus universalis librorum, in omni facultate, linguaque insignium, & rarissimorum; non solum ex catalogis Bibliothecarum bodleianæ, lugduno-batavæ, ultrajectinæ, barberinæ, thuanæ, cordesianæ, tellerianæ, slusianæ, & heinsianæ, sed etiam ex omnibus fere aliis prælo impressis magno labore & sumptu in usum studiosorum collectus. Londini 1699. pp.[viii].175+159 + 40 + 192 + 128 + [ii].129–160 + 264 + 214 + 119+115[*sic*, 116]. [30,000.]
reissued in 1701.

[CHRISTIAN GOTTLIEB LUDOVICI], Bibliotheca nominalis cvriosa, seu notitia avtorvm et librorvm maximam partem nostri ævi. Vitembergae 1703. pp.[iv].283. [3500.]
reissued in [1705] as a so-called 'editio secunda'.
—— Continvatio. 1705. pp.[iv].216. [3000.]

[CLAUDE FRANÇOIS MÉNESTRIER], Bibliothèque curieuse et instructive de divers ouvrages anciens & modernes, de littérature & des arts. Trévoux 1704. pp.[xvi].164+229. [500.]

BURCARD GOTTHELFF STRUVE, Introdvctio ad [in] notitiam rei litterariæ ad vsvm bibliothecarvm. Ienæ 1704. pp.[viii].203.[ii].208. [1000.]

— — Editio secvnda. 1706. pp.[xv].576.[xlviii]. 76. [2000.]

— — — Svpplementa. 1710. pp.[iv].177.[x]. [250.]

— — [third edition]. 1710. pp.[xv].76.576. [xlviii]. [2000.]

this edition consists of a reissue of the 1706 edition and the 1710 supplements; the supplements alone were also reissued in 1716.

— — Editio qvinta. Francofvrti &c. 1719. pp. [xvi].969.[xcix]. [5000.]

— — Sextum prodit cura Io. Christiani Fischeri. Francofurti &c. 1754. pp.24.988.[lxv]. [6000.]

— — Bibliotheca historiae litterariae selecta, olim titvlo Introdvctionis in notitiam rei litterariae ... insignita ... post variorvm emendationes et additamenta opvs ita formavit vt fere novvm dici qveat Iohannes Fridericvs Ivgler. Ienae 1754–1763. pp.[xxiv].768 + [viii].769–1640 + [vi].1641–2274. [lxxxviii]. [7500.]

— — — Joannis Friderici Jugleri ... Supplementa et emendationes ... ex auctoris schedis manuscriptis edidit ... Hermann. Frider. Koecher. ... Fasciculus 1. Ienae 1785. pp.viii.339. [1350.]

ADOLPHUS CLARMUNDUS, Vitæ clarissimorum in re literaria virorum. Das ist: lebens-beschreibung etlicher hauptgelehrten männer, so von der Literatur profess gemacht. ... Altera editio. Wittenberg 1704–1707. pp.[x].237 + [vi].270 + 232 + 208. [xxx]+[vi].257+[vi].232. [2000.]
vol.iv contains an index to the first four volumes.

THOMAS CREMIUS [*pseud.* TH. TH. CRUSIUS], De singularibus scriptorum dissertatio epistolica ad juvenem . . . Mauricium Georgium Weidmannum. Lugduni in Batavis 1705. pp.128. [100.]

NEUE bibliothec oder nachricht und urtheile von neuen büchern. Franckf. &c.
    i. [By Wilhelm Türck]. 1709–1710. pp.916. [xxviii]. [1510.]
    ii. [By Nicolaus Hieronymus Gundling].
    iii.
    iv.
    v.

THE STUDENT's library: or, a choice collection of books in all faculties and parts of learning. 1713. pp.[iv].91. [3000.]

VINCENTIUS PARAVICINUS, Singularia de viris eruditione claris centuriæ tres. Basileæ 1713. pp.[viii]. 110.[*sic*, 210].[vi]. [2000.]

Bibliography

[NICOLAS BARAT], Nouvelle bibliothèque choisie, où l'on fait connoître les bons livres en divers genres de litérature et l'usage qu'on en doit faire. Amsterdam 1714.

the author's name is taken from the preface, but according to Auguste Bernus, Notice bibliographique sur Richard Simon (Bâle 1882], this bibliography is by Simon.

BENJAMIN HEDERICH, Notitia avctorvm antiqva et media, oder leben, schrifften, editiones und censuren der ... scribenten, so von anfange an, bis auf die instauration der studien im occidente, gelebet, und einem gelehrten zu kennen nützlich und nöthig seyn. Wittenberg 1714. pp.[xvi].1114. [xviii]. [5000.]

— — Känntniss der vornehmsten schriftsteller vom anfange der welt bis zur wiederherstellung der wissenschaften. Zwote ... ausgabe. [Edited by J. J. Schwabe or J. L. Warneyer]. Wittenberg &c. 1767. pp.[xvi].676+677–1412.[xvi]. [10,000.]

MYLES DAVIES, Athenæ britannicæ: or, a critical history of the Oxford and Cambridge writers and writings, with those of the dissenters and romanists, as well as other authors and worthies, both domestick and foreign, both ancient and modern.

1716. pp.[iv].88.348.[ix].+[viii].l.436.[x]+[vi].
12.112.56.24.40.40.32.[iv].14.8.8.[iv].12 + 4.8.
[68].24.28.[12].16.8.[8].4 + vi.120.2–6.[iii].ii.34.
22+8.58.24.56.24.40.32.28. [3000.]

the subtitle varies; the composition of this work varies almost from copy to copy; the book is made up of various pieces, including periodicals and verse, some of which were probably published independently; the title-pages of vols. iv–vi bear no date; vol. [ii] bears no volume-number; vol. i is a reissue of the author's anonymous Εἰκων μικρο-βιβλικη, *and vol. ii is largely a continuation of that work, which is entered under Broadsides: General, below.*

GOTTLIEB STOLLE, Kurtze anleitung zur historie der gelahrheit. Halle im Magdeburgischen 1718. pp.[xv].423.[xxix] + [ii].280.[xiv] + [ii].221.[ix]. [4000.]

—— Anleitung [&c.] . . . nunmehr zum dritten-mal . . . herausgegeben. Jena 1727. pp.[xv].778. [lxx]. [5000.]

——— Neue zusätze. 1727. pp.[viii].96.[xxiv]. [500.]

——— Ganz neue zusätze. 1736. pp.296. [1000.]

——— Introdvctio in historiam litterariam. . . . Latine vertit . . . Carolvs Henricvs Langivs. Ienae 1728. pp.[xx].xv.892.[cxiv]. [5000.]

Bibliography

CONRAD SAMUEL SCHURZFLEISCH, Élogia scriptorvm illvstrivm et mvlta ervditionis copia insignivm secvli XVI. Vittembergae 1729. pp.[x].96.
[500.]

[JEAN PIERRE NICERON], Mémoires pour servir à
l'histoire des hommes illustres dans la république
des lettres. Avec un catalogue raisonné de leurs
ouvrages. 1729–1745. pp.[xvi].382.[xviii] + [viii].
403.[xvii] + [xvi].378.[xiii] + [xvi].378.[xiii] +
[iv].416.[xii]. + [viii].408.[xvi] + [viii].411.[xiii]
+ [xii].408.[xvi] + [viii].408.[xv] + [viii].410.
[xiii] + [iii].xvi.190.clxxiii + [viii].316.xx + [vi].
405.[xvi] + [viii].406.[xvi] + [viii].408.[xiii].[vi].
401.[xviii] + [viii].409.[xiv] + [vi].410.[xiii] +
[viii].408.[xv] + [vi.411.[xiii] + [vi.408.[xiii] +
[iii].174.cl + [vi].411.[xiv] + [vi].410.[xiv] +
[vi].412.[xii] + [vi].408. [xiv] + [vi].410.[xiii] +
[vi].408.[xiv] + [vi].407. [xvi] + [vi].410.[xii] +
[viii].410.[xiv] + [vi]. 230.cxlxxx[sic, cxc].[iii] +
[xvi].410.[vi] + [xx].408.[iv] + [xx].408.[iv] +
[xx].407.[iv] + [xviii].409.[v] + [xx].408.[iv] +
[xx].405.[vi] + [xxiv]. 407.[iv] + [xxiv].406 +
[xxiv].396.[viii] + [xxiv].408 + [xxiv].404 +
[xxiv].406. [25,000.]

the author's name appears on the titlepages of vols.
xxx–xlv; indexes to vols. i–x, xi–xx, xxi–xxx appear
in vols. x, xx, xxx respectively; each of the succeeding

volumes contains a briefer index to the whole work to date; the Mémoires *are not arranged in any particular order.*

————Joh. Pet. Nicerons Nachrichten von den begebenheiten und schriften berühmten [*sic*] gelehrten mit einigen zusätzen herausgegeben von Siegmund Jacob Baumgarten [vols.xvi–xxii: FriedrichEberhardRambach;xxiii:ChristianDavid Jani]. Halle 1749–1771. pp.[xvi].552+[xxiv].464 + [xvi].464 + [xvi].500 + [xxiv].526 + [xxii]. 388 [*sic*, 488] + [xxiv].472 + [xxxii].446 + [xxx]. 480 + [xxviii].516 + [xxx].434 + [xxxviii].418 + [xxxii].440 + [xxiv].448 + [xiv].424 + [xxxii] 432 + [xxxviii].462 + [xl].438 + [xlvi].408 + [lxviii].426 + [xlviii].392 + [xxxii].392 + [xxiv]. 496. [25,000.]

c[ONRAD] s[AMUEL] SCHURZFLEISCH, Notitia scriptorvm librorumque uarii argumenti, quam ex uariis ipsius praelectionibus, in inclyta ad Albim academia ... habitis, studiose diligenterque collegit et edidit I.C. [part.iii: Godofredvs VVagenervs.] Vittembergae 1735–1738. pp.[ii].126 + [ii]. 62 + [ii].96.[xiv]. [500.]

————[another edition]. Notitia [&c.] [parts ii–iii: Introdvctio in notitiam scriptorvm ... studio Godofredi VVageneri]. Vittembergae 1737 [part

ii: 1736]. pp.[ii].126+[ii].426[*sic*, 526]+[ii].416.
[lx].158.[xiv]. [2000.]

part i of this edition is a reissue of part i of the 1735
edition; only one editor was concerned, for the initials
were a pseudonym.

THE LITERARY magazine: or the history of the
works of the learned. Containing an account of
the most valuable books publish'd both at home
and abroad, in most of the languages in Europe,
and in all arts and sciences. . . . By a society of
gentlemen [Ephraim Chambers *and others*].
[i]. 1735. pp.[vi].539.[viii]. [100.]
ii. 1736. pp.[vi].468.[vi]. [100.]
[*continued as:*]
The history of the works of the learned.
1737. pp.[iii].470.viii+[viii].469.xi. [200.]
1738. pp.[vi].456.[viii]+[ii].457.[vii]. [200.]
1739. pp.[iv].459.[vii]+[iii].458.[vi]. [200.]
1740. pp.[ii].458.[viii]+[ii].458.[viii]. [200.]
1741. pp.[vi].462.[viii]+[iv].475.[ix]. [200.]
1742. pp.[ii].459.[vii]+[ii].479.[vii]. [200.]

GABRIEL WILHELM GÖTTEN, Das jetzt lebende gelehrte Europa, oder nachrichten von den vornehmsten lebens-umständen und schriften jetzt
lebender europäischer gelehrten. Braunschweig
[vol.iii: Zelle] 1735–1740. pp.[xlviii].832.[viii] +

[xxxvi].818.[x] + [xxvi].224.[xvi].225–400.[iv].
401–652.[iv].653–876. [10,000.]

—— Geschichte jetztlebener gelehrten, als eine
fortsetzung des Jeztlebenden gelehrten Europa.
[By] Ernst Ludewig Rathlef [parts ix–xii: Johann
Christoph Strodtmann]. Zelle 1740–1747. pp.[xii].
292 + [iii].293–576 + [iv].282.[ii] + [iv].283–566
+ [iv].268 + [iv].269–548 + [xvi].240 + [viii].
241–504 + [xvi].240 + [xvi].241–480 + [xii].244 +
[viii].241–488.[xxiv]. [5000.]

—— Beyträge zur historie der gelahrtheit,
worinnen die geschichte der gelehrten unserer
zeiten beschrieben werden. [By Johann Christoph
Strodtmann *and others*]. Hamburg 1748–1750. pp.
[x].288.[viii] + [viii].264 + [iv].268.xvi + [iv].284
+[xvi].255. [2000.]

—— Das neue gelehrte Europa, als eine fortsetzung der dreyen werke, die bisher unter den
auffschriften, Gelehrtes Europa, Geschichte der gelehrten und Beyträge zur historie der gelahrtheit,
ans licht gestellet worden. Herausgegeben von
Johann Christoph Strodtmann [parts ix–xx: (Ferdinand Stosch)]. Wolfenbüttel [parts xix–xxi:
Braunschweig &c.]. 1752–1781. pp.[viii].280 +
[vi].281–570 + [vi].593–866 + [vi].881–1146 +
[vi].274 + [iv].275 + 544 + [iv].547–821 + [xii].
853–1078.[xviii] + [xii].248.[iv] + [viii].257–518.

74

[ii] + [viii].529–774.[ii] + [viii].785–1062 + [viii].
272 + [viii].281–560 + [viii].565–830 + [iv].839–
1073.[xvii] + [ii].250.[iv] + xvi.251–487.[iii] +
[viii].491–804.[iii] + [iv].809–1249 + [ii].1253–
1534. [20,000.]
the pagination is erratic.

GOTTLIEB STOLLE, Anmerckungen über d. Heumanns Conspectvm reipvblicae literariae. Jena
1738. p..[viii].1072.[civ]. [10,000.]
the Conspectus *itself is not a bibliography.*

THESAVRVS bibliothecalis: das ist: versuch einer
allgemeinen und auserlesenen Bibliothec, darinnen... ein accurates verzeichnis von allerhand alten
und neuen . . . in den vortreflichst . . . bibliothe-
quen, mit augen selber angesehen büchern. No-
rimbergæ 1738. pp.400+[iv].380.[xvi]. [1500.]

JACOB BRUCKER and JOHANN JACOB HAID, Bilder-
sal heutiges tages lebender, und durch gelahrheit
berühmter schrifft-steller; in welchem . . . ihre
lebens-umstände, . . . und schrifften aus glaub-
würdigen nachrichten erzählet werden. . . . Erstes
[–Zehentes und letztes] zehend. Augspurg 1741–
1755. pp.[550]. [2500.]

CHRISTIAN GOTTLOB JÖCHER, Allgemeines gelehrten-lexicon, darinne die gelehrten aller stände

. . . welche vom anfange der welt . . . gelebt, . . .
nach ihrer geburt, leben, . . . schrifften . . . beschrieben werden. Leipzig 1750–1751. pp.[xviii].
coll.2284.[x]. + pp.[iv].coll.2636.[viii]. + pp.[ii].
coll.2338.[x] + pp.[iv].coll.2250.[viii]. [50,000.]

—— Beytrag zum Jöcherischen Gelehrtenlexi-
con. Von Ernst Christian Hauber. Kopenhagen
&c. 1753. pp.48. [160.]

—— Fortsetzung und ergänzungen . . . von
Johann Christoph Adelung [vols.iii–vi: von Heinrich Wilhelm Rotermund]. Leipzig [vols.iii: Del-
menhorst; iv–vi: Bremen] 1784–1819. pp.[xvi].
coll.2496 + pp.[ii].coll.2364 + pp.vi.coll.vii–
lxxxii.2208 + pp.iv.coll.v–x.2200 + pp.vi.coll.
vii–x.2200+pp.vii.coll.2200. [200,000.]

A–Rinov only; no more published by the author.

—— Einige zusätze und verbesserungen.
[*c.*1810–1816]. coll.cccxvi. [2000.]

*published in three parts, referring respectively to
vols.iii–v of the Fortsetzung.*

—— Beiträge zur ergänzung und berichtigung
des Jöcher'schen Allgemeinen gelehrten lexikon's
und des Mensel'schen Lexikon's der von 1750 bis
1800 verstorbenen teutschen schriftsteller. Von
Karl August Hennicke. Leipzig 1811-1812. pp.iv.
92+[iv].108+[ii].122. [3000.]

—— Siebenter band. Mit einem anhang enthaltend die für die 2. ausgabe des 3. bandes (K) bestimmten verbesserungen und zusätze aus dem handexemplar des verfassers . . . herausgegeben von Otto Günther. Deutsche gesellschaft: Leipzig 1897. pp.vii.coll.724. [10,000.]

the continuation, Rinswerger-Romuleus, is also printed from the author's ms.

— — Johann Gottlob Wilhelm Dunkels Historisch-kritische nachrichten von verstorbenen gelehrten und deren schriften insonderheit aber denienigen, welche in der allerneuesten ausgabe des Jöcherischen Allgemeinen gelehrten-lexicons entweder gänzlich mit stillschweigen übergangen, oder doch mangelhaft und unrichtig angeführet werden. Cöthen [and Dessau] 1753–1759. pp. [xxii].348 + 349–735[xxix] + 228 + 229–392 + 393–584 + [xxiv].587–768.[xxvi] + [xvi].244 + 245–434+435–634+635–888. [15,000.]

— — Anhang von zusätzen und anmerkungen. [By — Schlichter]. 1760. pp.889–1132. [1000.]

BIBLIOTHÈQUE annuelle et universelle. . . . Contenant un catalogue de tous les livres qui ont été imprimés en Europe pendant l'année. [By Paul Denis Burtin and Jean Baptiste Ladvocat].

　i. 1748. 1751. pp.xxxiv.[vi].336. [600.]
　ii. 1749. 1752. pp.xxiv.488. [1000.]

iii. 1750. 1753. pp.xii.314 + [iii].315–685. [lxxiv]. [1500.]
no more published.

[JEAN BAPTISTE] LADVOCAT, Dictionnaire historique portatif contenant l'histoire des patriarches . . . des papes, des ss. pères, des évêques, . . . des historiens, poètes . . . et mathématiciens, etc. avec leurs principaux ouvrages et leurs meilleures éditions. 1752. pp.[vi].viii.501.78.[vi]+[iii].700.[ii]. [4000.]

a copy in the Bibliothèque nationale contains ms. notes; several times reprinted.

— — Dictionnaire historique et bibliographique portatif. . . . Nouvelle édition. 1777. pp.xxiii. 706.[vi].x.x + [iv].344.434.[iii].viii.viii + [ii].840. [vi].xii.8. [7500.]

— — — Supplément. [By J. P. Deforis]. 1789. pp.iv.696. [2000.]

— — Nouvelle édition, . . . où l'on a fondu le supplément de Le Clerc. 1822. pp.[vi].480+[iii]. 473+[iii].575+[iii].474+[iii].496. [10,000.]

Le Clerc was the publisher of the 1789 supplement.

— — Dictionnaire historique, philosophique et critique. . . . Nouvelle édition revue . . . et continuée jusqu'en 1789 par une société de savans, de littérateurs et de bibliographes. 1821–1822. pp.xiv.480+ [iii].473+[iii].575+[iii].474+[iii].496. [5000.]

——Dictionnaire classique des hommes célèbres de toutes les nations ... abrégé de Ladvocat et de Feller par E. Hocquart. 1822.

——Dizionario storico portatile. ... Edizione novissima ... col supplemento ... di Giangiuseppe Origlia ... e colle note del p. d. Anton Maria Lugo. Bassano 1773.

——Historiai dictionariuma. ... Magyar nyelvre fordította ... Mindszenti Sámuel. Komaromban 1795–1797. pp.x.596+[ii].483+[ii].514+[ii].470+[ii].662+[viii].624. [5000.]

———[Supplement]. Pozsonyban 1808–1809. pp.[vi].287+[iii].332. [1000.]

——An historical and biographical dictionary. ... Translated ... by Catharine Colignon. Cambridge 1799–1801. pp.[437]+[466]+[566]+[438]. [5000.]

JOHANN HEUMANN, Apparatvs ivrisprvdentiae literarivs. Norimbergae 1752. pp.[xii].386.[xvi]. [1000.]

the title is misleading.

GEORG CHRISTOPH HAMBERGER, Zuverlässige nachrichten von den vornehmsten schriftstellern vom anfange der welt bis 1500. Lemgo 1756–1764. pp.[xvi].220.596 + [vi].922 + [viii].824 + [xvi].843.[liii]. [20,000.]

— — Kurze nachrichten von den vornehmsten schriftstellern vor dem sechszehnden jahrhundert, in einem auszuge aus seinem grössern werke. 1766–1767. pp.[xvi].1888.[xiv]. [14,000.]

PROSPER MARCHAND, Dictionnaire historique, ou mémoires critiques et littéraires, concernant la vie et les ouvrages de divers personnages distingués, particulièrement dans la république des lettres. La Haye 1758–1759. pp.[iii].336 + [vi].328. [xxxviii]. [5000.]

ANNALES typographiques, ou notice du progrès des connoissances humaines; ... Par une société de gens de lettres.
    [1758]. 1760. pp.576+703. [1000.]
    [1759]. 1761. pp.576+650. [1200.]
    [1760].
    [1761]. 1762. pp.576+627. [1200.]
    [1762]. 1763. pp.576+580. [1200.]

JOHANN CHRISTOPH STOCKHAUSEN, Critischer entwurf einer auserlesenen bibliothek für die liebhaber der philosophie und schönen wissenschaften. ... Dritte ... auflage. Berlin 1764. pp.xl.408. [1500.]
    — Vierte ... auflage. 1771. pp.xxxii.672. [2000.]

CHRISTOPHORUS SAXIUS [CHRISTOPH GOTTLOB SAXE], Onomasticon literarivm, sive nomenclator

historico-criticvs praestantissimorvm omnis aeta-
tis, popvli artiumq. formvlae scriptorvm...Editio
altera. Traiecti ad Rhenvm.

    i. Scriptores . . . graecos et latinos usque ad
       . . . annum . . . 475 edens. 1775. pp.xlii.598.
       [6000.]

    ii. Usque ad . . . annum . . . 1499 aperiens.
       1777. pp.[ii].660. [6500.]

    iii. Usque ad saeculi xvi annum 85 . . . edens.
       1780. pp.[ii].x.660. [6500.]

    iv. Usque ad saeculi xvii annum 51 . . . edens
       1782. pp.[ii].659. [6500.]

    v. Usque ad annum 1700 . . . edens. 1785.
       pp.[ii].655. [6500.]

    vi. Usque ad . . . saeculi [annum] 39 . . . exhi-
       bens. 1788. pp.[ii].744.[iv].47. [7500.]

    vii. Usque ad . . . saeculi annum 74 . . . exibens.
       1790. pp.ix[*sic*, xix].448. [4500.]

    viii. Nomenclator scriptorum . . . qui vel
       superstites adhuc sunt vel nuper decesse-
       runt. 1803. pp.viii.464. [4500.]

    —— Onomastici literarii epitome. Trajecti
    ad Rhenum 1792. pp.[iii].190.

*an index of authors; there does not appear to have
been an earlier edition.*

ALLGEMEINES verzeichnis neuer bücher mit kur-

zen anmerkungen. [Edited by Christian Daniel
Beck]. Leipzig.

    [i]. 1776. pp.768. [2000.]
    ii. 1777. pp.[iv].1036. [2500.]
    iii. 1778. pp.[ii].1048. [2500.]
    iv. 1779. pp.[iv].1012. [2500.]
    v. 1780. pp.[iv].1016. [2500.]
    vi. 1781. pp.1011. [2500.]
    vii. 1782. pp.999. [2500.]
    viii. 1784. pp.1000. [2500.]

[JOHANN NEPOMUK COSMAS MICHAEL] DENIS,
Einleitung in die bücherkunde. Wien 1777–1778.
pp.[xiv].277+[viii].423. [2500.]
—— [another edition]. Bingen 1782. pp.xvi.
368+
—— Zweyte . . . ausgabe. Wien 1795–1796.
pp.[xvi].293+[vii].498. [3000.]
——— Bibliografia. . . . Traduzione con
aggiunte eseguita . . . dall'abate Antonio Roncetti.
Milano 1846. pp.[ii].v.365. [3000.]

ALLGEMEINES autor- und litteraturlexikon . . . bis
1778. Hannover 1778. pp.368. [4000.]
A–G only; no more published.

HEINRICH WILHELM LAWÄTZ, Handbuch für
bücherfreunde und bibliothekare. Halle 1788–

1795. pp.[ii].xxviii.692.[ii] + [ii].xvi.762.[iv] +
[iii].xvi.620+[iv].viii.788+[v].606+[ii].xiv.884
+[iii].1156. [35,000.]

incomplete; no more published.

—— Dreyfaches register zu den drey ersten
bänden des ersten theiles. 1791. pp.[iii].400.

—— Erster nachtrag zu den drey ersten bänden
des ersten theiles. 1791. pp.xxxvi.490+[ii].xx.506.
[7672.]

—— Zweyter nachtrag [&c.].1794. pp.[ii].xxii.
352. [2782.]

—— Erster nachtrag zum vierten bande des
ersten theiles. 1792. pp.[vi].418. [4000.]

*the fourth volume and its supplement were also issued
separately; see under Biography, below.*

GIORNALE de' libri nuovi delle più colte nazioni
dell' Europa. Milano.

    [i]. 1789. pp.[208]. [1500.]
    [ii]. 1790. pp.[208]. [1500.]
    [iii]. 1791. pp.[208]. [1500.]

CARL JOSEPH BOUGINÉ, Handbuch der allgemeinen litteraturgeschichte, nach Heumanns Grundriss. Zürich 1789–1792. pp.xvi.632+[ii].708+[ii].
718+[ii].774+viii.726. [25,000.]

—— Des ersten supplement bandes erster

[zweiter] theil. 1800–1802. pp.[ii].422+[ii].421. [8000.]

JOHANN JOACHIM ESCHENBURG, Lehrbuch der wissenschaftskunde; ein grundriss encyklopädischer vorlesungen. Berlin &c. 1792. pp.[xvi].351. [2500.]

[JOHANN SAMUEL ERSCH], Allgemeines repertorium der literatur. Jena [1791–1800: Weimar].
    [i]. 1785–1790. 1793–1794. pp.[vii].22.[580] +[556]+xii.410.35.52.78. [25,000.]
    [ii]. 1791–1795. 1799–1800. pp.[782]+[iii].12. [742]+viii.262.224.56. [25,000.]
    iii. 1796–1800. 1807. pp.viii.[606]+[552].115. 17. [12,500.]
no more published.

[JOHANN FRIEDRICH] LUDWIG WALCHER, Versuch einer allgemeinen geschichte der litteratur. Lemgo 1793–1796. pp.xvi.566 + [xvi].552 + [vi].940. [7500.]

— — [another edition]. Handbuch der allgemeinen geschichte der literärischen cultur. Marburg 1804–1805. pp.xvi.492 + xi.493–1184. [15,000.]

— — Zweyte umarbeitung. Handbuch der geschichte der litteratur. Frankfurt a. M. 1822–1824. pp.[ii].x.298 + [ii].v.296 + [vi].378 + xiii.384. [10,000.]

—— Dritte umarbeitung. Leipzig 1833. pp.xv.
416+v.463+iv.514+v.491. [15,000.]

FRIEDRICH CARL GOTTLOB HIRSCHING [vols.viii-
xvii: JOHANN HEINRICH MARTIN ERNESTI], Histo-
risch-literarisches handbuch berühmter und denk-
würdiger personen, welche in dem 18. jahrhunderte gestorben sind. Leipzig.

   i. [A–Deshays]. 1794–1795. pp.[ii].xii.402+
    [ii].382. [6000.]

   ii. Desig–Hartshöfer. 1795–1796. pp.[ii].402
    +[ii].370. [6000.]

  iii. Hartzheim–Kreitmayr. 1797. pp.[ii].354+
    [ii].382. [5000.]

  iv. Kremer–Marperger. 1799. pp.[ii].366+
    [ii].366. [5000.]

   v. Marschall–Mustapha. 1800. pp.[ii].334+
    [ii].221. [4000.]

  vi. Nad–Pagendarm. 1804. pp.[ii].402+[ii].
    382. [5000.]

 vii. Pagenstecher–Placette. 1805. pp.[ii].422+
    [ii].390. [5000.]

viii. Placidus–Räm. 1806. pp.[ii].408+[ii].
    390. [4000.]

  ix. Räthel–Ritter. 1806-1807. pp.[ii].366+[ii].
    365. [4000.]

   x. Rivalz–Schellenberg. 1807-1808. pp.[ii].
    370+[ii].384. [4000.]

xi. Scheller-Schwarzkopf. 1808. pp.[ii].385+
[ii].410. [4000.]

xii. Schwebel-Sperling. 1809. pp.[ii].366+
[ii].426. [4000.]

xiii. Spiegel-Sutor. 1809. pp.[ii].386+[ii].
390. [4000.]

xiv. Suvée-Trippel. 1810. pp.[ii].376+[ii].
382. [4000.]

xv. Tröltsch-Wasse. 1812–1813. pp.[ii].404+
[ii].401. [4000.]

xvi. Wateau-Wutgenau. 1813–1815. pp.[ii].
374+[ii].384. [4000.]

xvii. Wyermann-Zurlauben. 1815. pp.[ii].
306. [1500.]

AUGUST BURKARDT [*pseud.* JOHANN GEORG
HEINZMANN], Anleitung zur bücherkunde in allen
wissenschaften. Grundlage zu einer auserlesenen
bibliothek in allen fächern. Bern 1797. pp.391.
[xxiii]. [4000.]

IMMANUEL VERTRAUGOTT ROTHE, Die kunst, sich
eine bibliothek zu sammlen und zu ordnen; oder
systematisches verzeichniss der besten schriften aus
allen wissenschaften und künsten. Ronneburg
1798. pp.xxxvi.508. [2000.]

JOHANN GEORG MEUSEL, Leitfaden zur geschichte der gelehrsamkeit. Leipzig 1799–1800.

pp.xvi.420.[ii] + [ii].421–870 + [ii].871–1356.
[10,000.]

L[OUIS] DUTENS, Bibliothèque complette et choisie, dans toutes les classes et dans la plupart des
langues. Londres. 1800. pp.[ii].ii.32. [500.]

— — Seconde édition. Londres 1805. pp.[ii].ii.
33. [600.]

JOURNAL général de la littérature étrangère, ou
indicateur bibliographique et raisonné des livres
nouveaux en tous genres, cartes géographiques,
gravures et œuvres de musique qui paraissent dans
les divers pays étrangers à la France. [Edited by
Philipp Werner Loos].

   i. 1801. pp.[ii].4.288+[ii].289–576. [1500.]
   ii. 1802. pp.[ii].288+[ii].289–576. [1500.]
   iii. 1803. pp.[ii].288+[ii].289–576. [1500.]
   iv. 1804. pp.[ii].288+[ii].289–576. [1500.]
   v. 1805. pp.[ii].288+[ii].289–480. [1500.]
   — Répertoire complet des cinq premières
     années. [1805]. pp.481–648.
   vi. 1806. pp.[ii].288+[ii].289–576. [1500.]
   vii. 1807. pp.[iv].384. [1500.]
   viii. 1808. pp.[iv].384. [1500.]
   ix. 1809. pp.[iv].384. [1500.]
   x. 1810. pp.[ii].288. [1000.]

Bibliography

— Répertoire complet des années 1806 à
1810. [1810]. pp.165.

xi. 1811. pp.[ii].384. [1500.]

xii. 1812. pp.[ii].384. [1500.]

xiii. 1813. pp.[ii].384.16. [1500.]

xiv. 1814. pp.[ii].384. [1500.]

xv. 1815. pp.[iii].288. [1000.]

— Répertoire complet des années 1811 à
1815. [1815]. pp.116.

xvi. 1816. pp.[iv].384. [1500.]

xvii. 1817. pp.[iv].384. [500.]

xviii. 1818. pp.[ii].384. [500.]

xix. 1819. pp.[ii].386. [500.]

xx. 1820. pp.[iv].288. [1000.]

— Répertoire complet des années 1816 à
1820. [1820]. pp.156.

xxi. 1821. pp.[ii].370. [1500.]

xxii. 1822. pp.[iv].384. [1500.]

xxiii. 1823. pp.[iv].384. [1500.]

xxiv. 1824. pp.[iv].384. [1500.]

xxv. 1825. pp.[iv].288. [1000.]

— Répertoire complet des années 1821 à
1825. [1825]. pp.188.

xxvi. 1826. pp.[iv].384. [1500.]

xxvii. 1827. pp.[iv].384. [1500.]

xxviii. 1828. pp.[iv].384. [1500.]

xxix. 1829. pp.[iv].384. [1500.]

xxx. 1830. pp.[iv].256. [1000.]

— Table méthodique . . . 1825 à 1830. pp. 257–532.

[*continued as:*]

Journal général de la littérature de France. . . . Bulletin de la littérature étrangère.

1831. pp.[ii].136. [1000.]

1832. pp.[ii].154. [1250.]

1833. pp.[ii].144. [1250.]

1834. pp.[ii].152. [1250.]

1835. pp.[ii].[128]. [1250.]

1836. pp.[ii].168. [1500.]

1837. pp.[ii].176. [1500.]

1838. pp.[ii].176. [1500.]

1839. pp.[ii].176. [1500.]

1840. pp.[ii].160. [1500.]

1841. pp.[ii].168. [1500.]

no more published; the indexes of the first series were reissued under the title of Bibliographie étrangère.

w. d. führmann, Die merkwürdigsten und verdienstvollsten personen der alten und neuen zeit, in kurzen biographischen und literarischen nachrichten . . . gesammelt. Leipzig 1805–1808. pp.xii. 356+iv.362+358. [5000.]

johann gottfried eichhorn, Geschichte der litteratur von ihrem anfang bis auf die neuesten

zeiten. Göttingen 1805–1811. pp.xvii.918+[ii].
xxii.522 + 523–984 + xii.719 + xii.720–1297 +
[iii].508 + [ii].viii.509–1116 + [iii].1117–1448 +
xviii.678+[ii].xiv.532+[ii].xvi.794. [20,000.]

HEINRICH PERTSCH, Neues allgemeines litera-
risch-artistisches lexikon. Coburg &c. 1807. pp.
xii.468+xvi.376. [4000.]

SAMUEL BAUR, Neues historisch-biographisch-
literarisches handwörterbuch von der schöpfung
der welt bis zum schlusse des achtzehnten jahrhunderts. Ulm 1807–1810. pp.xvi.coll.990+pp.
[ii].coll.972 + pp.[ii].coll.860 + pp.[ii].coll.972 +
pp.xvi.coll.992. [20,000.]

GIORNALE bibliografico universale. Milano.
   i. 1807. pp.[ii].384. [1000.]
   ii. 1808. pp.384. [1000.]
   iii. 1808. pp.384. [1000.]
   iv. 1809. pp.384. [1000.]
   v. 1809. pp.384. [1000.]
   vi. 1810. pp.344. [1000.]
   — Indice generale . . . vol. I al. VI. pp.li.
   vii. 1810. pp.384. [1000.]
   viii. 1811. pp.384. [1000.]
   ix. (nos.1-2). 1811. pp.192. [500.]
no more published.

SAMUEL BAUR, Allgemeines historisch-biogra-

phisch-literarisches handwörterbuch aller merk-
würdigen personen, die in dem ersten jahrzehend
des neunzehnten jahrhunderts gestorben sind. Ulm
1816. pp.x.coll.864+pp.[ii].coll.768. [5000.]

[ÉTIENNE] GABRIEL PEIGNOT, Traité du choix des
livres. 1817. pp.xx.295. [750.]

ALLGEMEINES repertorium der neuesten in- und
ausländischen literatur. Herausgegeben von einer
gesellschaft gelehrten. Leipzig.

[i]. 1819. pp.vi.382+[ii].398+[ii].406+[ii].
398+[ii].66. [2000.]

[ii]. 1820. pp.[ii].398+[ii].414+[ii].432+[ii].
432+iv.80. [2500.]

[iii]. 1821. pp.[ii].480+[ii].480+[ii].480+
[ii].480+[ii].84. [2500.]

[iv]. 1822. Besorgt von Christian Daniel Beck,
pp.[ii].480 + [ii].480 + [ii].480 + [ii].480
+[ii].92. [2500.]

[v]. 1823. pp.[ii].480+[ii].496+[ii].480+[ii].
480+[ii].74. [2500.]

[vi]. 1824. pp.[ii].480+[ii].480+[ii].456+[ii].
392+[ii].54. [2500.]

[vii]. 1825. pp.[ii].480+[ii].480+[ii].392+
[ii].386+[ii].60. [2500.]

[viii]. 1826. pp.[ii].480+[ii].480+[ii].116 [*sic*,
416]+[ii].400+[ii].61. [2500.]

[ix]. 1827. pp.[ii].480+[ii].480+[ii].448+
[ii].414+[ii].62. [2500.]

[x]. 1828. pp.[ii].482+[ii].480+[ii].416+[ii].
392+[ii].50. [2500.]

[xi]. 1829. pp.[ii].480+[ii].480+[ii].384+
[ii].384+[ii].42. [2000.]

[xii]. 1830. pp.[ii].480+[ii].480+[ii].448+
[ii].384+[ii].42. [2000.]

[xiii]. 1831. pp.[ii].480+[ii].480+[ii].384+
[ii].384+[ii].48. [2000.]

[xiv]. 1832. pp.[ii].480+[ii].480+[ii].26.
[1000.]

[continued as:]

Neues allgemeines repertorium . . . Redaction
von Karl Heinrich Ludwig Pölitz.

xv. 1833. pp.[ii].480+[ii].480+[ii].480+[ii].
480+[ii].48. [2500.]

replaced by the Repertorium der gesammten
deutschen literatur, *which is entered under German
literature, below; the present series was accompanied
by an* Intelligenzblatt, *afterwards* Bibliographischer
anzeiger. . . . Intelligenzblatt, *which is in the nature
of an advertisement sheet.*

[ANTOINE ALEXANDRE BARBIER], Examen critique
et complément des dictionnaires historiques . . .
Tome 1er, (A-J). . . . Par l'auteur du Dictionnaire

des ouvrages anonymes et pseudonymes. 1820.
pp.[iii].viii.492. [2500.]

no more published.

[SIR SAMUEL EGERTON BRYDGES], Polyanthea
librorum vetustiorum, italicorum, gallicorum,
hispanicorum, anglicanorum, et latinorum. Pars I.
Genevæ 1822. pp.lvi.464. [1000.]

no more published, but the book is complete as it
stands; 75 copies printed.

[ÉTIENNE PSAUME], Dictionnaire bibliographique, ou nouveau manuel du libraire et de l'amateur de livres, contenant l'indication . . . de tous
les livres . . . qui peuvent trouver leur place dans
une bibliothèque choisie. Par m. P*****. 1824.
pp.264.264+[iii].507. [15,000.]

T[HOMAS] F[ROGNAL] DIBDIN, The library com-
panion; or, the young man's guide, and the old
man's comfort, in the choice of a library. 1824.
pp.[iii].lii.400+[ii].512. [3000.]

— — Second edition. 1825.

a Specimen, *limited to historical works and entered*
below under History: Miscellaneous, was published in
1810.

J. F. ROLLAND, Conseils pour former une bibliothèque, ou catalogue raisonné de tous les bons

ouvrages qui peuvent entrer dans une bibliothèque chrétienne. Lyon 1833–1843. pp.viii.464+viii.623 +[iii].548. [17,632.]

L[OUIS] AIMÉ MARTIN, Plan d'une bibliothèque universelle. . . . Suivi du catalogue des chefs-d'œuvre de toutes les langues. Bruxelles 1837. pp. [iii].545. [1500.]

BIBLIOGRAPHIE universelle. Résumé périodique des publications nouvelles de tous les pays.
    [i]. 1838. pp.284.8.10.10.7. [4332.]
    ii. 1839. pp.308.10.20. [4331.]

[JOHANN] CHR[ISTIAN] FR[IEDRICH] HARLESS, Die litteratur der ersten hundert jahre nach der erfindung der typographie, in den meisten hauptfächern der wissenschaft. Leipzig 1840. pp.xviii.288. [1500.]

REVUE de bibliographie analytique, ou compte rendu des ouvrages scientifiques et de haute littérature, publiés en France et à l'étranger.
    i. 1840. pp.1183. [1250.]
    ii. 1841. Par [Emmanuel Clément Bénigne] Miller et [A.] Aubenas. pp.1184. [1000.]
    iii. 1842. pp.1186. [1250.]
    iv. 1843. pp.1184. [1500.]
    v. 1844. pp.1184. [1500.]

vi. 1845. pp.1160. [1000.]
no more published.

LEIPZIGER repertorium der deutschen und ausländischen literatur. Unter mitwirkung der uni-
versität Leipzig herausgegeben von E[phraim]
G[otthelf] Gersdorf. Leipzig.

    i. 1843. pp.[vi].580+[vi].572+[vi].592+[vi]
      604+96. [9500.]

    ii. 1844. pp.[vi].564+[vi].536+[vi].536+
      [vi].560+116. [10,500.]

    iii. 1845. pp.[vi].544+[vi].552+[vi].520+
      [vi].520+124. [11,500.]

    iv. 1846. pp.[vi].520+[vi].528+[vi].516+
      [vi].544+120. [11,000.]

    v. 1847. pp.[vi]528+[vi].520+[vi].528+[vi].
      560+116. [11,000.]

    vi. 1848. pp.[vi].508+[vi].484+[vi].436+
      [vi].424+88. [7500.]

    vii. 1849. pp.[iii].iv.384+[iii].380+[iii].372
      +[iii].320+68. [5500.]

    viii. 1850. pp.[iii].388+[iii].376+[iii].344+
      [iii].356. [5500.]

    ix. 1851. pp.352+336+336+368. [5500.]

    x. 1852. pp.382+[iii].360+366+373. [4500.]

    xi. 1853. pp.[vi].376+[vi].368+[vi].368+
      [vi].384. [5500.]

xii. 1854. pp.[vi].368+[vi].376+[vi].368+
[vi].383. [5500.]

xiii. 1855. pp.[vi].368+[vi].368+[vi].368+
[vi].368. [6000.]

xiv. 1856. pp.[vi].368+[vi].368+[vi].368+
[vi].388. [5500.]

xv. 1857. pp.[vi].360+[vi].360+[vi].368+
[vi].372. [5500.]

xvi. 1858. pp.[vi].368+[vi].368+[vi].368+
[vi].391. [6000.]

xvii. 1859. pp.[vi].368+[viii].368+[vi].368
+[vi].375. [5500].

xviii. 1860. pp.[ii].360+[vi].360+[vi].360+
[vi].362. [5000.]

no more published; this publication replaced the
Repertorium der gesammten deutschen literatur,
*which is entered under German Literature: Nineteenth
century, below.*

REVUE bibliographique de l'année. Par Ch[arles]
P[oisson]. Vouziers [printed].

1845. pp.118. [300.]
1846. 1847. pp.219. [600.]
no more printed.

[D. APPLETON & CO.], Appleton's library manual;
containing a catalogue raisonné of upwards of
twelve thousand of the most important works in
every department of knowledge, in all modern

languages. New-York &c. 1847. pp.iii–xvi.434. [12,000.]

reissued in [1847] *with a London imprint under the title of* A library manual.

—— [another edition]. Edited by Thomas Delf. 1852–1854.

[EUSÈBE] GIRAULT DE SAINT-FARGEAU, Histoire littéraire française et étrangère, ou analyse raisonnée des œuvres choisies de tous les écrivains qui se sont fait un nom dans les sciences et les lettres. 1852. pp.viii.422. [2000.]

—— Deuxième édition. 1852. pp.[vi].498. [2000.]

REVUE bibliographique. Bulletin analytique des principales publications de la France et de l'étranger. No.1er. 1856. pp.48. [200.]

ALLGEMEINE bibliographie. Monatliches verzeichniss der wichtigen neuen erscheinungen der deutschen und ausländischen literatur. [Vols.i–vii: By] Paul Trömel. Leipzig.

    i. 1856. pp.xl.220. [3915.]
    ii. 1857. pp.xxxix.200. [3603.]
    iii. 1858. pp.xxxix.216. [3806.]
    iv. 1859. pp.xxxix.216. [3729.]
    v. 1860. pp.xl.216. [4003.]

vi. 1861. pp.xxxix.192. [3398.]

vii. 1862. pp.xxxix.176. [3118.]

viii. 1863. pp.xliii.168. [3303.]

ix. 1864. pp.xlvi.168. [3488.]

x. 1865. pp.l.216. [4225.]

xi. 1866. pp.xxxvi.184. [3444.]

xii. 1867. pp.xxxv.192. [3265.]

xiii. 1868. pp.xxxiv.192. [3171.]

xiv. 1869. pp.xxxviii.192. [3444.]

xv. 1870. pp.xxxix.192. [3489.]

xvi. 1871. pp.xli.192. [3469.]

xvii. 1872. pp.xxxix.192. [3532.]

xviii. 1873. pp.xl.192. [3707.]

xix. 1874. pp.xli.192. [3670.]

xx. 1875. pp.xlii.192. [3591.]

xxi. 1876. pp.xli.192. [3579.]

xxii. 1877. pp.xl.192. [3603.]

xxiii. 1878. pp.xlii.192. [3665.]

xxiv. 1879. pp.xliv.192. [3712.]

xxv. 1880. pp.xlii.192. [3679.]

xxvi. 1881. pp.xlvi.192. [3731.]

xxvii. 1882. pp.xlvii.192. [3792.]

xxviii. 1883. pp.xlvi.192. [3936.]

xxix. 1884. pp.xliv.192. [4006.]

xxx. 1885. pp.xlvi.192. [4175.]

xxxi. 1886. pp.xlvi.192. [4218.]

xxxii. 1887. pp.xliv.192. [4212.]

xxxiii. 1888. pp.xlviii.192. [4641.]
xxxiv. 1889. pp.xlviii.192. [4812.]
xxxv. 1890. pp.xlviii.192. [4709.]
xxxvi. 1891. pp.xlviii.192. [4747.]
xxxvii. 1892. pp.xlviii.192. [4804.]
xxxviii. 1893. pp.xlviii.192. [4670.]
xxxix. 1894. pp.xlviii.192. [4719.]
xl. 1895. pp.xlviii.192. [4746.]
xli. 1896. pp.xlviii.192. [4599.]
xlii. 1897. pp.xlviii.192. [4612.]
xliii. 1898. pp.xlviii.192. [4576.]
xliv. 1899. pp.xlvi.192. [4639.]
xlv. 1900. pp.xlvi.192. [4758.]

xlvi. 1901. pp.xlvi.192. [4718.]
xlvii.1902. pp.xlviii.192. [4911.]
xlviii. 1903. pp.xlviii.192. [4910.]
xlix. 1904. pp.xlviii.192. [4903.]
l. 1905. pp.xlviii.192. [4900.]
li. 1906. pp.xlvi.192. [4785.]
lii. 1907. pp.xlvi.192. [4747.]
liii. 1908. pp.xliv.192. [4659.]
liv. 1909. pp.xliv.192. [4662.]

[continued as:]

Brockhaus' allgemeine bibliographie [&c.],
Monthly list. . . . Bibliographie universelle.

lv. 1910. pp.192. [4781.]
lvi. 1911. pp.192. [4832.]

lvii. 1912. pp.102. [4919.]
lviii. 1913. pp.102. [5000.]
lix. 1914. pp.192. [5000.]
lx. 1915. pp.192. [5000.]
no more published.

FERDINAND [JEAN] DENIS, P[IERRE] PINÇON and [GUILLAUME FRANÇOIS] DE MARTONNE, Nouveau manuel de bibliographie universelle. Manuels-Roret: 1857. pp.xi.706. [40,000.]
a copy in the Bibliothèque nationale contains ms. additions; also issued in three volumes.

G[USTAVE] VAPEREAU, Dictionnaire universel des contemporains, contenant toutes les personnes notables de la France et des pays étrangers, avec . . . leurs écrits et les indications bibliographiques qui s'y rapportent. 1858. pp.[iii].xi.1803. [20,000.]
— — Supplément. 1859. pp.46.[l]. [2500.]
consists partly of corrected leaves of the main work.
— — Deuxième édition. 1861. pp.[iii].xi. 1840. [20,000.]
— — Troisième édition. 1865. pp.[iii].x.1863. [20,000.]
— — Quatrième édition. 1870. pp.[iii].iv. 1888. [20,000.]
— — Cinquième édition. 1880. pp.[iii].viii. 1892.lxviii. [20,000.]

—— Sixième édition. 1893. pp.[iii].iv.1631. [30,000.]

——— Supplément. 1895. pp.[iii].ii.103. [1000.]

A[LFRED] DANTÈS, Tables biographiques et bibliographiques des sciences, des lettres et des arts, indiquant les œuvres principales des hommes les plus connus en tous pays et à toutes les époques. 1866. pp.vii.646.[ii]. [125,000.]

V[LADIMIR] I[ZMAILOVICH] MEZHOV, Исторія русской и всеобщей словесности. Библіографическіе матеріалы, расположенные въ систематическомъ порядкѣ и касающіеся литературъ: русской и другихъ славянскихъ нарѣчій, западно-европейскихъ, сѣверо-американской, классической и восточной и появившихся въ свѣтъ на русскомъ языкѣ, какъ отдѣльными сочиненіями, такъ и статьями въ періодическихъ изданіяхъ, за послѣдніе 16 лѣтъ, т. е. съ 1855 до 1870 года, включительно. С.-Петербургъ 1872. pp.xxiii. 708.[ii]. [15,705.]

ALFRED DANTÈS, Dictionnaire biographique et bibliographique . . . des hommes les plus remarquables . . . chez tous les peuples, à toutes les époques. 1875. pp.1423+157. [100,000.]

Bibliography

[COUNT] A[NGELO] DE GUBERNATIS, Dizionario biografico degli scrittori contemporanei. Firenze 1879[-1880]. pp.xxxii.1276. [40,000.]

—— [another edition]. Dictionnaire international des écrivains du jour. Florence 1888–1891. pp.1042+8.1043–2088. [75,000.]

WILLIAM A[DOLPHUS] WHEELER, Who wrote it? An index to the authorship of the more noted works in ancient and modern literature. Boston 1881. pp.[ii].174. [3500.]

FRANZ BORNMÜLLER, Biographisches schriftsteller-lexicon der gegenwart. . . . Die bekanntesten zeitgenossen auf dem gebiet der nationalliteratur aller völker mit angabe ihrer werke. Meyers fach-lexika: Leipzig 1882. pp.vi.800. [20,000.]

G. BORNHAK, Lexicon der allgemeinen litteratur-geschichte. Die nationallitteratur der ausserdeutschen völker. Meyers fach-lexika: Leipzig 1882. pp.[iv].520. [5000.]

F[REDERICK] LEYPOLDT and LYNDS E. JONES, The books of all time. A guide for the purchase of books. New York 1882. pp.80. [750.]

W[ILLIAM] M[CCRILLIS] GRISWOLD, An index to articles relating to history, biografy [sic], literature, society, and travel contained in collections of essays (etc.). Q. P. indexes (no.xiii). Bangor [Maine] 1883. pp.56. [4000.]

—— Second edition. 1884. pp.xx.11–56.[iv]. [4000.]

THE BEST books. A list for the guidance of general readers.... By an old book-lover. Sheffield 1886. pp.28. [500.]

WISSENSCHAFTLICHE bibliographie der weltlitteratur. No.1[–12]. Leipzig 1887. pp.272. [7500.]
no more published.

WILLIAM SWAN SONNENSCHEIN. The best books. A reader's guide. 1887. pp.xvi.713. [25,000.]

—— Second edition. 1891. pp.[xii].cix.1009. [50,000.]
reissued with corrections in 1894, 1896, 1901, 1903.

——— First supplement. A reader's guide to contemporary literature. 1895. pp.15.lxxiv.775. [20,000.]
reissued in 1901.

—— Third edition. 1910–1935. pp.[iii].459+ [v].461–1065+[v].1067–1679+[iv].1681–2510+ [iv].2511–3385+lii.3385–3760. [150,000.]

FRANK PARSONS, F. E. CRAWFORD and H. T. RICHARDSON, The world's best books. A key to the treasures of literature. Boston 1889. pp.vii.134. [large number.]

C[ARLOS] FRONTAURO and M[ANUEL] OSSORIO
Y BERNARD, *edd*. Diccionario biográfico inter-
nacional de escritores y artistas del sigle XIX. . . .
Tomo primero. Madrid 1890. pp.[iv].918.
[20,000.]
A–D only; no more published.

I[VAN] I[VANOVICH] YANZHUL [*and others*],
Книга о книгахъ. Толковый указатель
для выбора книгъ по важнѣйшцмъ. Москва
1892. pp.xx.289+x.176. [5000.]

CHARLES [ANTOINE] GIDEL and FRÉDÉRIC LOLIÉE,
Dictionnaire-manuel-illustré des écrivains et des
littératures. Bibliothèque de dictionnaires-ma-
nuels-illustrés: 1898. pp.[iv].908. [20,000.]

R[UTHERFORD] P[LATT] HAYES, Reference cata-
logue.for readers. Short lists of the best books.
Chicago [1899]. pp.32. [1000.]

FRANK W[ALTER] RAFFETY, Books worth reading.
1899. pp.[xiii].174. [250.]

CLASS list of $500 library recommended for
schools. New York state library: Bulletin (no.65:
Bibliography no.30): Albany 1901. pp.955–1032.
[1000.]

HENRY CARNOY, *ed*. Dictionnaire biographique
international des écrivains. Collection des grands

dictionnaires biographiques: [1902–]1909. pp.vi.
264+264+208+210. [10,000.]

JOHN M[ACKINNON] ROBERTSON, Courses of
study. 1904. pp.viii.516. [2500.]
— — Third edition. 1932. pp.xii.526. [7500.]

THE INTERNATIONAL bibliographer.... A monthly register & record of modern culture. Vol.1. no.1
[–2]. 1910. pp.56. [1500.]
no more published.

LIST of editions of ancient and modern classic
authors (including translations). Library of Congress: Washington 1909. ff.34. [176.]*

ZAIDEE BROWN, Buying list of books for small
libraries. New York state library: Albany 1910.
pp.40. [900].
— — Sixth edition. Compiled by Marion Hor-
ton. American library association: Chicago 1940.
pp.viii.143. [1800.]

GUIDE DE LECTURE, Répertoire bio-bibliogra-
phique. Catalogue de la bibliothèque choisie. 2ᵉ
édition. Bruxelles &c. [1911]. pp.31.lxxx.1032.
[30,000.]

STANDARD books. An annotated and classified
guide to the best books in all departments of
literature. [General editor, F. C. Tweney]. [1911].

pp.992+792+920+[v].655. [20,000.]
some sheets were revised in 1912–1915 without disturbing the pagination.

LIST of series of standard and classic authors. Library of Congress: Washington 1916.ff.2. [16.]★

BESSIE GRAHAM, The Bookman's manual. New York 1921. pp.xi.434. [4000.]
— — 9th edition. The reader's adviser.... Revised ...by HesterR. Hoffman. 1960.pp.xix.1116. [10,000.]

HELEN REX KELLER, The reader's digest of books New York 1924. pp.[iv].941. [2000.]

[HENRY TOOD COSTELLO], A list of books for a college student's reading. Trinity college: Hartford 1925. pp.99. [900.]
— — Fifth edition. Books for a college [&c.]. 1958. pp.vi.133. [1000.]

OUVRAGES remarquables parus dans différents pays au cours de l'année 1925. Société des nations: Institut international de coopération intellectuelle: 1927. pp.47. [750.]

RAYMOND PEARL, To begin with. Being prophylaxis against pedantry. New York &c. 1927. pp.[xi].96. [75.]

Bibliography

J[OHN] BARTLET BREBNER [*and others*], Classics of the western world. American library association: Chicago 1927. pp.128. [1500.]
—— Third edition. 1943. pp.146. [1500.]

LES MEILLEURS livres dans la plupart des domaines du savoir humain. Bruxelles [1929]. pp.80. [3000.]

LEONARDO. Rassegna bibliografica. Anno 1. Milano 1930. pp.840. [5000.]
no more published; forms a supplement to the Nuova antologia *and* I libri del giorno.

EUGENE HILTON, Junior college book list. University of California: Publication in education (vol.vi, no.1): Berkeley 1930. pp.[iv].84. [2000.]

CHARLES B[UNSEN] SHAW, A list of books for college libraries. . . . Second preliminary edition. American library association: Chicago 1931. pp. [ii].xii.810. [14,000.]
—— Supplement. Books for catholic colleges. . . . Compiled . . . by Melania Grace . . . and Gilbert C[harles] Peterson. pp.x.134. [2000.]*
——— Supplement.*
    1948–1949. pp.[vi].57. [750.]
    1950–1952. Compiled . . . by Melania Grace . . .
    and Louis A. Ryan. pp.vi.55. [700.]

1953–1955. Compiled . . . by Melania Grace and Eugene P. Willging. pp.vi.64. [900.]

ALUMNI reading lists. University of Michigan: Ann Arbor.

   [i]. 1931. pp.xii.155. [1250.]

   ii. 1934. By Edith Thomas and T. R. Barcus. pp.xi.209. [2000.]

      [*continued as:*]

What to read. Alumni reading lists.

   iii. 1939. [By E. Thomas, Fred. L. Dimock and Nelis R. Kampenga]. pp.[ii].xii.285. [3000.]

WHO's who among living authors of older nations except . . . America. Edited by A. Lawrence. Volume I, 1931–1932. Los Angeles [1932]. pp.v.482. [40,000.]

R[OBERT] FARQUHARSON SHARP, A short biographical dictionary of foreign literature. Everyman's library (no.900): 1933. pp.303. [5000.]

R[OBERT] A[LEXANDER] PEDDIE, Subject index of books published before 1880. 1933. pp.xv.746. [40,000.]

   — — Second series. 1935. pp.xvi.858. [50,000.]

   — — Third series. 1939. pp.xvi.945. [40,000.]

a facsimile of the whole was issued, London 1962.

w. TARG, 999 books worth reading. A check-list of the world's best books. Chicago 1934. pp.43. [999.]

HENRIQUE PERDIGÃO, Dicionário universal de literatura (bio-bibliográfico e cronológico). Barcelona 1934. pp.xxiv.792. [15,000.]
—— Seconda edição. Porto 1940. pp.xxxv. 1043. [17,500.]

FRED EASTMAN, Books that have shaped the world. American library association: Chicago 1937. pp.63. [250.]

GEORGE W. COTTRELL and HOXIE N. FAIRCHILD, Critical guide prepared for the home study course in world literature [of Columbia university]. New York 1939. pp.xxvii.378. [2000.]

[HENRY LANCELOT DIXON], The 'quintessence' of literature. [Warminster 1940]. pp.[v].139. [500.]

STANLEY J[ASSPON] KUNITZ and HOWARD HAY-CRAFT, Twentieth century authors. New York 1942. pp.vii.1577. [50,000.]
—— First supplement. . . . Assistant editor Vineta Colby. 1955. pp.x.1123. [40,000.]

[MILFRED REFO CARR *and others*], The St. John's college list of great books. Enoch Pratt free library: Baltimore 1943. pp.36. [100.]

JAMES G[OODWIN] HODGSON, The world book encyclopediabibliography. Chicago [1943]. pp.24. [1200.]

CURRENT foreign literature. A monthly review of outstanding continental publications in all branches of literature. 1945.
no more published.

PIERRE [LOUIS] WIGNY, *ed.* La bibliothèque de l'honnête homme. Bruxelles 1945. pp.iii–xv.604. [3000.]
—— [another edition]. [1953]. pp.xix.675. [4000.]

HAVE you read 100 great books? New York [1946]. pp.80. [1000.]
— Third edition. [1950]. pp.144. [1000.]

LANDMARKS in world thought: a selected list of a hundred books. Library of Congress: Washington 1947. ff.14. [107.]*

[FREDERICK B. ADAMS *and others*], One hundred influential books printed before 1900. Catalogue. Grolier club: New York 1947. pp.140. [100.]

ERASMVS. Specvlvm scientiarvm. Amsterdam [Darmstadt].
in progress.

CATALOGUE méthodique des publications de la

Bibliography

'Documentation française'. Présidence du conseil: Direction de la documentation: 1948. pp.48. [1000.]

quarterly indexes are also issued.

OUVRAGES examinés par la Commission des livres du Ministère de l'éducation nationale. Education nationale (no.16, supplément): 1949. pp. xxiv. [700.]

CARL F. BRAUN, Two hundred good books. A list and reviews. Alhambra, Cal. 1949. pp.142. [200.]

JE CHOISIS . . . mes auteurs. [1950]. pp.317. [5000.]

SCRINIUM. Elenchus bibliographicus universalis. Pax romana: Fribourg/Suisse.

    i. 1950. pp.211. [3000.]
    ii. 1951. pp.420. [3200.]
    iii. 1952. pp.442. [2086.]
    iv. 1953. pp.432. [2474.]
    v. 1954. pp.362. [2357.]
    vi. 1955.

INTERNATIONAL P.E.N. bulletin of selected books. Issued in association with Unesco. 1950&c. *in progress.*

FRANCIS J[AMES] CARMODY and ARTURO TORRES-RIOSECO, Contemporary english, french and

spanish literature. A working guide (with brazil-
ian-portuguese). Dubuque 1951. pp.iv.ff.44.
[750.]*

E[RICH] FRAUWALLNER, H[ANS] GIEBISCH and
E[RWIN] HEINZEL, *edd*. Die welt-literatur. Biographisches, literarhistorisches und bibliographisches
lexikon in übersichten und stichwörtern. Wien
[1951–1954]. pp.xii.644 + [iv].645–1284 + [iv].
1285–2119. [25,000.]

NEUERSCHEINUNGEN wissenschaftlicher literatur
aus den ländern der volksdemokratie: Albanien,
Bulgarien, Polen, Rumänien, Tschechoslowakische
republik, Ungarn, volksrepublik China. Zentral-
stelle für wissenschaftliche literatur: Berlin.

    i. 1951–1952. pp.818. [7222.]
    ii. 1953. pp.1288. [6628.]*
    iii. 1954. pp.1284. [6612.]*
    iv. Januar–Juni 1955. pp.672. [2947.]*
no more published.

ASA DON DICKINSON, The world's best books,
Homer to Hemingway. New York 1953. pp.viii.
484. [3000.]

FRANK J. BERTALAN, Books for juniors colleges.
American library association: Chicago 1954.
pp.xiii.321. [4000.]

E[RWIN] HEINZEL, Lexikon historischer ereignisse und personen in kunst, literatur und musik. Wien [1956], pp.xxvii.782. [8000.]

BOOKS published abroad. . . . Books sponsored by book translation program. U. S. information agency. [Washington 1956 &c.].
loose-leaf.

DIZIONARIO letterario Bompiani degli autori di tutti i tempi e di tutte le letterature. Milano 1956–1957. pp.xv.832+xi.884+xi.956. [75,000.]
—— [another edition]. Dictionnaire biographique des auteurs de tous les temps et de tous les pays. [1957–1958]. pp.[iv].736+[ii].736. [50,000.]

AGUSTÍN YÁÑEZ, Los libros fundamentales de nuestra época. Guadalajara 1957. pp.45. [21.]

[A. M. GORBUNOV *and others*], К VI всемирному фестивалю молодежи и студентов. Рекомендательные списки художественной литературы и литературы об искусстве зарубежных стран. Государственная ордена Ленина библиотека СССР имени В. И. Ленина: Москва 1957. pp.112. [1200.]

B[ORIS] L[UOVICH] KANDEL, Путеводитель по иностранным библиографиям и спра-

вочникам по литературоведению и художественной литературе. Государственная...
библиотека им. М. Е. Салтыкова-Щедрина:
Ленинград 1959. pp.443. [1541.]

Z. V. ZHITOMIRSKAY [*and others*], Основные
произведения иностранной художественной
литературы. Литературно-библиографичес-
кий справочник. Всесоюзная государственная библиотека иностранной литературы:
Москва 1960. pp.599. [5000.]

SIR WILLIAM EMRYS WILLIAMS, *ed.* The reader's
guide. Pelican books (no.A500): Harmondsworth
1960. pp.351. [3000.]

CLIFTON FADIMAN, The lifetime reading plan.
Cleveland &c. [1960]. pp.320. [500.]

AN INDEX to book reviews in the humanities.
[Detroit].*
   i. 1960. pp.xii.408. [30,000.]
   ii. 1961. pp.xiv.443. [35,000.]
   iii. 1962. pp.xiii.344. [25,000.]

GERT A. ZISCHKA, Allgemeines gelehrten-lexi-
kon. Biographisches handwörterbuch zur geschichte der wissenschaften. Kröners taschenaus-
gabe (vol.306): Stuttgart [1961]. pp.viii.710.
[15,000.]

Bibliography

CONTEMPORARY authors. The international bio-bibliographical guide to current authors and their works. Detroit.

    i. James M. Ethridge, editor. [1962]. pp.246. [5000.]

    ii.

    iii. [1963]. pp.245. [5000.]

    iv. [1963]. pp.289. [5000.]

in progress.

CHARLES L. TRINKNER, *ed.* Basic books for junior college libraries. Northport, Ala. [1963]. pp.783. [20,000.]

HANNAH LOGASA, World culture. A selected, annotated bibliography. McKinley bibliographies (vol.iii): Philadelphia [1963]. pp.xiv.384. [6000.]

CHOICE. Books for college libraries. Association of college and research libraries: Chicago March 1964 &c.

in progress.

7. 'Bibliographic control'

CHARLES F. BALZ and RICHARD H. STANWOOD, Literature on information retrieval and machine translation. International business machines corporation: [White Plains, N.Y.] 1962. pp.ix.117. [3000.]*

Bibliography

MARSHALL SPANGLER, General bibliography on information storage and retrieval. General electric: Computer department: Technical information series (no.R62CD2): [Schenectady] 1962. pp. [vii].390. [1550.]*

PAUL C. JANASKE, *ed.* Information handling and science information. A selected bibliography, 1957–1961. American institute of biological sciences: Biological sciences communication project: Washington 1962. pp.[256]. [1121.]*

DOCUMENTATION & information retrieval. A selected bibliography. Western reserve university: Center for documentation and communication research: Cleveland [1962]. pp.8. [85.]*

8. *Miscellaneous*

i. *Lost and unique books*

J[OSEPH] M[ARIE] QUÉRARD, Livres perdus et exemplaires uniques. Œuvres posthumes . . . publiés par [Pierre] G[ustave] Brunet: Bordeaux 1872. pp.[iii].103. [250.]
   300 copies printed.

[PIERRE GUSTAVE BRUNET], Livres perdus. Essai bibliographique sur les livres devenus introuva-

bles. Par Philomneste Junior. Bruxelles 1882. pp.
ix.122. [400.]

500 copies printed.

A[RMAND] DELPY, Essai d'une bibliographie spé-
ciale des livres perdus, ignorés ou connus à l'état
d'exemplaire unique. 1906–1911. pp.[v].156+[iii].
175. [2219.]

100 copies printed; A–P only, no more published.

ii. 'Mad' books

CHARLES NODIER, Bibliographie des fous. De
quelques livres excentriques. Bulletin du bibliophile (no.21, supplément): 1835. pp.40. [20.]

[JOSEPH] OCTAVE DELEPIERRE, Histoire littéraire
des fous. London 1860. pp.[ii].184. [100.]

[PIERRE GUSTAVE BRUNET], Les fous littéraires.
Essai bibliographique sur la littérature excentrique,
les illuminés, visionnaires, etc. par Philomneste
Junior. Bruxelles 1880. pp.xi.227. [500.]

500 copies printed.

—— Rectifications et additions...par Av[gust]
Iv[anovich] Tcherpakoff [Cherpakov]. Moscou
1883. pp.90. [200.]

iii. *Unfinished and unpublished books*

THEODOOR JANSSON VAN ALMELOVEEN, Bibliotheca promissa et latens. Gandæ [1692]. pp.[xv]. 160. [750.]

the date appears as cIↃ IↃ cIIxc.

— — M. Rodolphi Martini Meelführeri Accessiones. Noribergæ &c. 1699. pp.[xvi].176. [1500.]

ALBERT R. CORNS and ARCHIBALD SPARKE, A bibliography of unfinished books in the english language. 1915. pp.xvi.256. [2500.]

300 copies printed.

MARINO PARENTI, Bibliografia di edizioni e opere incompiute. Firenze [1938–1951].

incomplete; no more published.

MORIZ GROLIG and MICHAEL O. KRIEG, Mehr nicht erschienen. Ein verzeichnis unvollendet gebliebener druckwerke. Bibliotheca bibliographica (vol.ii): Bad Bocklet &c. 1954–1958. pp.xvi.443 + xvi.471. [15,000.]

iv. *Miscellaneous*

TOBIAS MAGIRUS, Eponymologivm criticvm ex principum sacrorum, secularium, virorum togatorum, sagatorum, locorvm insignium, patrum, philologorum . . . medicorum . . . poëtarum, oratorum, historicorum descriptionibus, in utramque partem cognomentorum luxta [*sic,* juxta], quibus noti ac notati, varietate delenifica locupletiùs concinnatum. Francofurti ad Mœnum 1644. pp.[xx].253. [3000.]

—— Nunc duplo quàm olim auctius editum cura Christiani Wilhelmi Eybenii. Francofurti &c. 1687. pp.[viii].812. [5000.]

a copy containing numerous additions in ms. is in the British museum.

THÉOPHILE RAYNAUD, Erotemata de malis ac bonis libris. Lugduni 1653. pp.[xii].378.[xvii]. [600.]

JOHAN MÖLLER, Homonymoscopia historico-philologico-critica, sive schediasma παρεργικον de scriptoribus homonymis quadripartitum. Hamburgi 1697. pp.[xvi].970. [4000.]

ELIA DE AMATO, Museum literarium, in quo penè omnium scriptorum dubia, supposititia, maledica, falsa, fabulosa, satyrica, proscripta, anonyma, suffurata, insulsa, putidaque monumenta, eruditorum criterio, strictim expenduntur. Neapoli 1730. pp.383.[xxi]. [2000.]

JO[HANN] CHRISTIAN KLOTZ, De libris avctoribus svis fatalibvs liber singvlaris. Lipsiæ 1761. pp.208. [100.]

reprinted in 1768.

JOHN COLE, An ænigmatical catalogue of books

of merit, on an entirely new plan. Scarborough 1821. pp.44. [250.]

—— A key to Cole's Ænigmatical catalogue. 1821. pp.16.

the titles are suggested by riddles.

BIBLIOPOLISCHES und bibliographisches jahrbuch für 1842/43. Leipzig 1842. pp.xxv.272. [2500.]

A. DEREUME, Notices bio-bibliographiques sur quelques imprimeurs, libraires, . . . etc. qui se sont fait connaître . . . principalement comme auteurs. Bruxelles 1858. pp.[iii].65. [3000.]

100 copies printed.

[PIERRE GUSTAVE BRUNET], Les livres cartonnés. Essais bibliographiques par Philomneste Junior. Bruxelles 1878. pp.101. [300.]

500 copies printed.

LOUDOLPHE DE VIRMOND, Récréations bibliographiques. 1882. pp.[iii].187. [300.]

a select bibliography of works by early writers whose names are the same as those of modern french writers.

JAMES LYMAN WHITNEY, A modern proteus, or a list of books published under more than one title. New York 1884. pp.106. [400.]

FERNAND DRUJON, Essai bibliographique sur la

destruction volontaire des livres ou bibliolytie.
1889. pp.[iii].73. [270.]
256 copies printed.

[CARL FRIEDRICH WEGENER], Vorschlag zu einer
lesebibliothek für junge frauenzimmer.... Mit...
einem verzeichniss scherzhafter cataloge ... herausgegeben von Hugo Hayn. Borna 1889. pp.63.
[catalogues: 35.]
the latter part consists of a list of catalogues of
imaginary books.

P[ETER] H[AMPSON] DITCHFIELD, Books fatal to
their authors. Book-lover's library: 1895. pp.xx.
245. [200.]

GEO[RGE] A[RTHUR] STEPHEN, Books and reading
... a selection of english and american books in
print. Third edition. [National book council].
Bibliography (no.64): 1928. pp.[2]. [75.]

— [another edition]. [By Anne Cliff]. 1943.
pp.[4]. [60.]

PREPARATION of bibliographies. Library of Congress: Washington 1933. ff.4. [40.]*

KANG WOO [K'ANG WU], Histoire de la bibliographie chinoise. Institut des hautes études chinoises:
Bibliothèque: 1938. pp.iii–viii.131. [1000.]

Bibliography

[JOSEPH RUBINSTEIN and EARL FARLEY], He who destroyes a good booke, kills reason it selfe—an exhibition of books. University of Kansas: Libraries: Lawrence 1955. pp.28. [100.]

M. SCHUCHMANN, Bibliographie der normen für das gebiet der dokumentation. Fédération internationale de documentation: Publications (no. 303): La Haye 1958. pp.107. [1500.]

J[ULIE] L. DARGENT, Échanges internationaux de publications. Bibliographie 1817–1960. Commission belge de bibliographie: Bibliographia belgica (no.68): Bruxelles 1962. pp.[ii].iv.236+[ii].237–518. [2276.]*

Libraries, library science.

1. *Periodicals*

FLORENCE RISING CURTIS, List of library reports and bulletins in the collection of the University of Illinois Library school. University of Illinois: Bulletin (vol.ix, no.12): Urbana–Champaign 1912. pp.iv.22. [600.]

FLORENCE RISING CURTIS, List of library reports and bulletins in the collection of the university of Illinois Library school. University of Illinois: Bulletin (vol.ix, no.12): Urbana–Champaign 1912. pp.iv.22. [600.]

KATHARINE TWINING MOODY, Index to library reports. American library association: Chicago 1913. pp.185. [4000.]

SIGURD MÖHLENBROCK, Utländska biblioteks-tidskrifter. [Lund 1952]. pp.16. [50.]
— — Tredje ... upplagan. 1961. pp.66. [150.]

D. H. BORCHARDT, Union list of periodicals on

library science and bibliography held in the major libraries of Australia. University of Tasmania: Hobart 1953. pp.iv.25. [150.]*

UNION list of library periodicals. Contents in advance (vol.1, no.1–2): [Philadelphia] 1955. pp. [ii].22. [250.]*

[J. C. HARRISON], 100 periodicals for the librarian ... exhibited at the Library association annual conference. Library association: North-western branch: [Eccles] 1955. pp.[16]. [100.]

UNION LIST of library periodicals. Association of assistant librarians: South Wales and Monmouthshire division: 1956. ff.10. [60.]*
limited to the periodicals available in south Wales and Monmouthshire.

W. VAN DER BRUGGHEN, Library and documentation periodicals. International federation for documentation: Publication (no.295): The Hague 1956.
—— Second ... edition. ... (no.336): 1961. pp.30. [500.]

PHILLIPS [LUMSDEN] TEMPLE and JOHN HARVEY, A directory of library periodicals published in the continental United States. Kansas state college: Library: Pittsburg 1957. pp.iv.44. [700.]*

ПЕРИОДИЧЕСКАЯ печать СССР, 1917-1949. Библиографический указатель. Журналы, труды и бюллетени по вопросам печати, библиотечного дела и библиографии. Всесоюзная книжная палата: Москва 1959. pp.191. [1400.]

NÓMINA de publicaciones periódicas de bibliotecología y documentación existentes en la biblioteca. Universidad: Instituto bibliotecológico: Buenos Aires 1958. ff.[i].ii.20. [101.]*

HANS JÜRGEN ASCHENBORN, Biblioteekkundige tydskrifte in suid-afrikaanse biblioteke. Staatsbiblioteek: Bibliografieë (no.1): Pretoria 1960. ff.[31]. [200.]*

F. J. GUTHRIE, *ed.* Union list of professional periodicals . . . on librarianship held by scottish libraries. Association of assistant librarians: West of Scotland division: [1962]. pp.vi.19. [150.]*

NORMAN W. WOOD and ALAN G. THOMPSON, Union list of professional periodicals in northern libraries. Association of assistant libraries: Northeastern division: [1963]. pp.[16]. [100.]*

H[ERBERT] A[LLAN] WHATLEY, *ed.* Periodicals on librarianship held by special libraries in Scotland. Association of assistant librarians. Union list of professional periodicals: Supplement: [Perth] 1963. pp.[8]. [20.]

2. History

JOHANN CHRISTOPH KRÜSIKE, Vindemiarvm litterarvm specimen I, Qvo, de re libraria vniverse agitvr. . . . Accedit adpendix de scriptis rei bibliothecariae adfectis. Hambvrgi 1727. pp.40. [153.]

ERNST GUSTAV VOGEL, Literatur früherer und noch bestehender europäischer öffentlicher und corporations-bibliotheken. Leipzig 1840. pp.xvi. 548. [12,500.]

GUSTAV BECKER, Catalogi bibliothecarvm antiqvi. Bonnae 1885. pp.iv.330. [343.]
supplements appear in the Centralblatt für bibliothekswesen, *by M[ax] Perlbach (1885), ii.27–33, and by Gabriel Meier (1885), ii.239–241; (1887), iv.254–260, and in the* Deutsche literaturzeitung *(1885), col.79.*

THEODOR GOTTLIEB, Ueber mittelalterliche bibliotheken. Leipzig 1890. pp.xii.520. [1391.]
a bibliography of contemporary catalogues and documents; additions by Gabriel Meier appear in the Centralblatt für bibliothekswesen *(1903), xx. 16–32.*

FREDERICK J[OHN] TEGGART, Contribution towards a bibliography of ancient libraries. New York 1899. pp.13. [350.]

FREDERICK J[OHN] TEGGART, Librariana. An outline of the literature of libraries from the xivth to the xviith centuries. New York 1900. pp.13. [250.]

FRANCES SIMPSON, Syllabus for a course of study in the history of the evolution of the library in Europe and America. Champaign, Ill. 1903. pp.91. [250.]

BARBARA BRONSON, Bibliographical guides to the history of american libraries. University of Illinois: Library school: Occasional papers (no.32): [Urbana] 1953. pp.11. [150.]*

GIANETTO AVANZI, Libri, librerie, biblioteche nell'umanesimo e nella rinascenza. Cataloghi e notizie. Seconda edizione. Roma 1954. pp.20. [100.]

SEARS [REYNOLDS] JAYNE, Library catalogues of the english renaissance. Berkeley &c. 1956. pp. ix.225. [1000.]

[THOMAS SIDNEY MORGAN], Select bibliography on english library history for L. A. registration students. Hertford county council: Technical information service: [Hertford] 1960. pp.[12]. [77.]

Library Science

3. General

ANZEIGER für literatur der bibliothekswissen-schaft. [Edited by Julius Petzholdt]. Dresden &c. [1848–1855: Halle].

   1840. pp.iv.51. [89.]
   1841. pp.xviii.70. [104.]
   1842. pp.vi.92. [107.]
   1843. pp.xii.106. [135.]
   1844. pp.xvi.135. [183.]
   1845. pp.[vi].lviii.184. [624.]
   1846. pp.[vi].lxiv.194. [733.]
   1847. pp.iv.188. [624.]
   1848–1849. pp.iv.263. [811.]
         [continued as:]

Anzeiger für bibliographie und bibliotheks-wissenschaft.

   1850. pp.[iv].374. [1224.]
   1851. pp.[ii].374. [1549.]
   1852. pp.[ii].374. [1408.]
   1853. pp.[ii].376. [1330.]
   1854. pp.[ii].434. [1218.]
   1855. pp.[ii].420. [1133.]

after this volume the title was changed to Neuer anzeiger, *&c., and the journal took on a more general nature.*

[SAMUEL SWETT GREEN], Library aids. Bureau of education: Washington 1881. pp.10. [200.]

N. BOKACHEV, Описи русскихъ библіотекъ и библіографическія изданія, находящіяся въ исторической и археологической библіотекѣ Н. Бокачева. С.-Петербургъ 1890. pp.316.53.26. [919.]

READING list in library science. Part I. Bulletin of bibliography pamphlets (no.9): Boston 1902. pp. II. [150.]
no more published.

CATALOGUS der bibliographie en bibliotheconomie. Koninglijke bibliotheek: [The Hague] 1903. pp.[iii].76. [2405.]

BIBLIOGRAPHIE des bibliotheks- und buch-wesens. Leipzig 1904–1925.
          [*continued as:*]
Internationale bibliographie des buch- und bibliothekswesens. 1926–1940.
details of this work are entered under Bibliography, 1, above.

Ref. Room

H[ARRY] G[EORGE] T[URNER] CANNONS, Bibliography of library economy. 1910. pp.448. [20,000.]

√ —— 1876–1920. American library association: Chicago 1927. pp.680. [15,000.]

√ —— Supplement. Library literature, 1921–

1932. Compiled by the Junior members round table of the American library association under the editorship of Lucile M. Morsch. 1934. pp.xii.430. [10,000.]

[continued as:]

Library literature. An author and subject index-digest to current books, pamphlets and periodical literature relating to the library profession. New York.

> 1933–1935. Edited by Marian Shaw. pp.vii.
> 435. [5000.]
>
> 1936–1939. pp.xlviii.1748. [15,000.]
>
> 1940–1942. pp.xxx.1192. [10,000.]
>
> 1943–1945. Edited by Dorothy Ethlyn Cole.
> pp.xvi.309. [3500.]
>
> 1946–1948. pp.xxii.478. [5000.]
>
> 1949–1951. pp.xxvi.862. [8000.]
>
> 1952–1954. pp.xxv.809. [8000.]
>
> 1955–1957. pp.x.910. [9000.]
>
> 1958–1960. Edited by Helen Thornton Geer.
> pp.xv.687. [10,000.]

in progress; only the final cumulated issues are set out.

ANNA LORRAINE GUTHRIE, Library work. Cumulated 1905–1911. A bibliography and digest of library literature. Minneapolis 1912. pp.[iv].409. [2500.]

first published at irregular intervals, under the title of Library work, *from April 1906 to October 1911.*

A[UGUSTA] V[LADIMIROVNA] MEZIER, Словарный указатель по книговедению. Ленинград 1924. pp.xi.coll.926.pp.viii. [10,000.]

BUCH- und schriftwesen, bearbeitet von Friedrich Michael. Bibliothekswesen, bearbeitet von Hans Praesent. Jahresberichte des Literarischen zentralblattes über die wichtigsten wissenschaftlichen neuerscheinungen des gesamten deutschen sprachgebietes (1924, vol.i): Leipzig 1925. pp.85. [libraries: 200.]

M[IKHAIL] I[VANOVICH] SLUKHOVSKY, Указатель книг по библиотечному делу. Библиотечная база: Москва 1927. &c. pp.48. [123.]

THE YEAR's work in librarianship. Library association.

    i. 1928. Edited by Arundell Esdaile. pp.vii. 216. [500.]
    ii. 1929. pp.viii.260. [600.]
    iii. 1930. pp.[viii].207. [500.]
    iv. 1931. pp.[viii].296. [600.]
    v. 1932. pp.[viii].197. [500.]
    vi. 1933. pp.[viii].222. [600.]
    vii. 1934. pp.[viii].211. [750.]

viii. 1935. Edited by A. Esdaile and J. H. P. Pafford. pp.[x].290. [750.]

ix. 1936. pp.[x].264. [600.]

x. 1937. pp.x.322. [1000.]

xi. 1938. pp.x.339. [1000.]

xii. 1939–1945. Edited by J. H. P. Pafford. 1949. pp.x.452. [1500.]

xiii. 1946. 1949. pp.x.221. [750.]

xiv. 1947. Edited by W. A. Munford. 1951. pp.x.337. [1000.]

xv. 1948. 1952. pp.x.281. [750.]

xvi. 1949. 1952. pp.x.230. [700.]

xvii. 1950. 1954. pp.x.270. [750.]

[*continued as:*]

Five years' work in librarianship.

1951–1955. By P. H. Sewell. 1958. pp.viii. 418. [3000.]

1956–1960. 1963. pp.viii.559. [2000.]

in progress.

CURRENT library literature 1929–1930. New York 1931. pp.[iv].41. [750.]

OBRAS existentes en la biblioteca Colón de la Unión panamericana sobre organización de bibliotecas y sistemas de clasificación. Unión panamericana: Serie bibliográfica (no.8): Washington 1933. ff.13. [125.]*

MARGARET [HILDA] BURTON and MARION E[LEA-
NOR] VOSBURGH, A bibliography of librarianship.
Classified and annotated guide to the library
literature of the world (excluding slavonic and
oriental languages). Library association: 1934. pp.
[vi].176. [1750.]

DOROTHY CHARLES, Dissertations, theses, and
papers of the Graduate library school, university
of Chicago, 1930–1945. A bibliography. [Chicago
1945]. ff.[ii].28.[iv]. [132.]*

H. C. TWAITS, A catalogue of the library. Association of assistant librarians: [1949]. pp.18. [400.]

YA. PRAISMAN, Учет и охрана библиотечных фондов. Аннотированный указатель ос-
новной литературы. Академия наук Укра-
инской ССР [&c.]: Киев 1950. pp.40.

LIBRARY science abstracts. Library association.
 i. 1950. Edited by C. B. Muriel Lock and
  Reginald Northwood Lock. pp.46.280.
  [611.]
 ii. 1951. pp.42.296. [952.]
 iii. 1952. pp.47.284. [912.]
 iv. 1953. pp.40.284. [777.]
 v. 1954. pp.35.288. [841.]
 vi. 1955. pp.48.53.76.72.68. [1179.]

vii. 1956. pp.48.72.70.77.72. [1176.]
viii. 1957. pp.44.312. [1124.]
ix. 1958. pp.44.300. [1092.]
x. 1959. pp.51.334. [1088.]
xi. 1960. pp.54.359. [1004.]
xii. 1961. pp.56.352. [969.]
xiii. 1962. pp.56.372. [987.]
xiv. 1963. pp.56.400. [1053.]
in progress.

ROBERT B[INGHAM] DOWNS, American library resources. A bibliographical guide. American library association: Chicago 1951. pp.[xi].428. [5578.]*

LIST of bibliographies and theses accepted for part III of the university of London diploma in librarianship between 1936 and 1950. University of London: School of librarianship and archives: Occasional publications (no.1): 1951. pp.10. [150.]*
— [another edition]. Cumulated list of bibliographies and theses accepted for part II . . . 1946–1960. . . . (no.10): 1960. pp.[iv].37. [299.]*

CATALOGUS documentatie en bibliotheekwezen. Openbare leeszaal en bibliotheek: Enschede 1951. pp.[ii].coll.32. [750.]*

BIBLIOGRAPHY and librarianship. A select list. Public libraries: Bermondsey 1953–1954. pp.132. [1000.]*

A. G. KARIMULLIN, Доклады и сообщения на библиотечных семинарах. Казань 1955. pp.15. [75.]

БИБЛИОГРАФИЯ библиотековедения. Аннотированный указатель. Государственная... библиотека СССР имени В. И. Ленина: Москва 1956. &c.

PETER JONIKAS, Bibliography of public library surveys contained in the collections of the university of Chicago library and the headquarters library of the American library association. Chicago 1958. ff.21.[vii]. [280.]*

СВОДНЫЙ систематический каталог иностранных книг по библиотековедению. Академия наук СССР [&c.]: Ленинград.

    i. 1917–1945. [By N. A. Laskeev and T. I. Skripkina]. 1962. pp.135. [1062.]
    ii. 1946–1956. 1958. pp.83. [601.]
in progress.

BOOKS and pamphlets on library science in the Science museum library. Science library: Bibliographical series (no.769): [1959]. pp.12. [300.]*

BOLETÍN de adquisiciones de la biblioteca de la Escuela interamericana de bibliotecología. Medellín 1959 &c.★

in progress.

БИБЛИОТЕКОВЕДЕНИЕ и библиография. Указатель литературы. Государственная библиотека СССР имени Ленина: Москва 1959 &c.

in progress; details of this work are entered under Bibliography, above.

THE LITERATURE of library technical services. A survey of the publications in the fields of interest of the Resources and technical services division made by the Division's publications committee. University of Illinois: Library school: Occasional papers (no.55): Urbana 1960. pp.48.

FOCUSING on the library's public. Backbone books for a trustee's library. New York depart of education: Library trustees foundation of New York state: Albany 1961. ff.[ii].18. [50.]★

N. A. LASKEEV and T. I. SKRIPKINA, Сводный систематический каталог иностранных книг по библиотековедению. Академия наук СССР: Москва 1962.

[FRANÇOISE MALET and PAULE SALVAN], Bibliographie commentée à l'intention des candidats au diplôme supérieur de bibliothécaire. Direction des bibliothèques de France: 1962. pp.[iv].67.46. [400.]★

BASIC library general reference, cataloging, and book selection titles. Federal aviation agency: Library branch: Bibliographic list (no.2): Washington 1962. ff.i.8. [100.]★

DICTIONARY catalog of the library of the School of library service, Columbia university. Boston 1962.

    i. A–Brd. pp.[vi].836. [17,556.]
    ii. Bre–D. pp.[ii].837–1756. [19,299.]
    iii. E–H. pp.[ii].1757–2564. [16,947.]
    iv. I–L. pp.[ii].2565–3522. [19,887.]
    v. M–Per. pp.[ii].3523–4336. [17,073.]
    vi. Pes–St. pp.[ii].4337–5264. [19,467.]
    vii. Su–Z. pp.[ii].5265–6086. [17,241.]

this is a photographic reproduction of the catalogue cards; the numbers in square brackets refer to these cards.

4. Countries

Africa

A. G. LE SUEUR, Bibliographic guide to south african librarianship. University of Cape Town: School of librarianship: Bibliographical series:

Cape Town 1953. pp.x.149+[iv].37+iv.12.39. [1000.]*

HELEN F[IELD] CONOVER, African libraries, book production, and archives. A list of references. Library of Congress: General reference and bibliography division: Washington 1962. pp.vi.64. [341.]*

America, latin

ARTHUR ERIC GROPP, Bibliografía sobre las bibliotecas nacionales de los países latinoamericanos y sus publicaciones. Unión panamericana: Departamento de asuntos: Bibliographic series (no.50): Washington 1960. pp.iv.58.

Austria

ÖSTERREICHISCHE bibliographie des bibliothekswesens. Zeitschrift des Österreichischen vereins für bibliothekswesen [: Supplement : Wien &c.
1909–1910. pp.[ii].28. [350.]
[*continued as:*]
Österreichische und ungarische bibliographie &c.
1910–1911. pp.[ii].44. [540.]
1911–1912. pp.[ii].20. [258.]
1912–1913. pp.14. [201.]
no more published.

Library Science

Belgium

AUGUSTE COLLARD, La bibliothéconomie en Belgique, 1901–1925. Malines 1927. pp.36. [300.]

Brazil

BIBLIOGRAFÍA bibliotecológica brasileira. Biblioteca central: São Paulo 1952. pp.41.

OSWALDO DE CARVALHO, Bibliografia brasileira de biblioteconomia. (Edição preliminar). São Paulo 1959. pp.ix.97. [994.]*

Canada

CANADIAN library literature index. A preliminary check-list. Canadian library association: Ottawa 1956. pp.iv.79. [3000.]*

Colombia

BIBLIOGRAFÍA bibliotecológica colombiana. Manuales de bibliografía y documentación colombianas (no.1): Bogotá.

1953–1955. Recogida por Luis Florén [Lozano]. pp.57. [381.]
[*continued as:*]
Bibliografía bibliotecológica y bibliográfica colombiana.

1956–1958. pp.[vii].35. [235.]★
in progress.

Cuba

BIBLIOGRAFÍA bibliotecológica cubana. Biblioteca del bibliotecário (no.1 &c.): Habana.
1948. Por Elena Verez, Fermin Peraza
[Sarousa]. . . . (vol.i). ff.77. [500.]
1949. . . . (no.31). ff.[iv].71. [500.]
1950. . . . (no.34). ff.28. [183.]
1951. . . . (no.40). ff.40. [220.]
1952. . . . (no.39). ff.32. [168.]
1953. . . . (no.41). ff.37. [223.]
1954. . . . (no.42). ff.41. [259.]
1955. . . . (no.46). ff.34. [163.]
100 copies reproduced from typewriting.

Czechoslovakia

MARIE L. ČERNÁ, Soupis české a slovenské knihovnické literatury z let 1945–1955. Universita: Knihovna: Čteme a studujeme (1956, no.10): Praze 1956. pp.108. [1000.]

Denmark

E[RIK] ALLERSLEV JENSEN and TORBEN NIELSEN, Dansk bibliotekslitteratur. Bidrag til en biblio-

grafi. Under medvirken af Viggo Bredsdorff og
Else Nygaard. København 1950. pp.xvi.194.26.
[3000.]

Dominica

L[UIS] FLORÉN LOZANO, Bibliografía bibliotecológica dominicana, 1930–mayo 1952. Materiales
para el estudio de la cultura dominicana (no.8):
Ciudad Trujillo 1952. pp.28. [175.]

France

R[ENÉ] DE SAINT-MAURIS, Bibliographie et bibliothèques populaires. Société bibliographique: 1879.
pp.12. [13.]

ULYSSE ROBERT, État des catalogues de bibliothèques publiques de France. [*c*.1885]. pp.27.
[300.]

BULLETIN des biblothèques de France. Ministère
de l'Éducation nationale: Direction des bibliothèques de France.
  i. 1956. pp.1010. [1553.]
  ii. 1957. pp.1058. [1639.]
  iii. 1958. pp.1108. [1751.]
  iv. 1959. pp.600.638. [1891.]
  v. 1960. pp.495.590. [1523.]
*in progress; the scope of this publication is fairly
wide.*

Library Science

Germany

JULIUS PETZHOLDT, Literatur der saechsischen bibliotheken. Dresden &c. 1840. pp.xviii.54. [1000.]

A. GRAESEL, Special-katalog der bibliotheks-ausstellung. Deutsche unterrichts-ausstellung in Chicago: Berlin 1893. pp.x.44. [500.]

HANS TREBST, Die kataloge der grösseren bibliotheken des deutschen sprachgebietes. Ausschuss für sachkatalogisierung: Berlin 1935. pp.xv.188. [350.]

Hungary

FOLYÓIRATOK, hirlapok 1902. deczember 31-ig a Budapesti egyetemi könyvtár folyóirati szobájában. Budapest 1902. pp.101. [2000.]

Italy

LE BIBLIOTECHE governative italiane nel MDCCCXCVIII. Notizie storiche, bibliografiche e statistiche. Roma 1900. pp.vii.464. [400.]

CARLO FRATI and ALBANO SORBELLI, Dizionario bio-bibliografico dei bibliotecari e bibliofili italiani dal sec. XIV al XIX. Biblioteca di bibliografia italiana (vol.xiii): Firenze 1933. pp.[ii]. viii.707. [6000.]

— — Marino Parenti, Aggiunte al Dizionario [&c.]. Firenze 1952–1960. pp.3–310+3–278+3–258. [9000.]

333 copies printed.

1 CATALOGHI delle biblioteche italiane. Roma [1934]. pp.[392]. [2500.]

the text of this volume is made up of 27 offprints rom Accademie e biblioteche d'Italia (*1927–1933*).

E. APOLLONI and G. ARCAMONE, Le biblioteche d'Italia fuori di Roma. Storia, classificazione, funzionamento, contenuto, cataloghi, bibliografia. Bibliothèque des 'Annales institutorum' (vol. iii): Roma.

    i. Italia settentrionale. Parte prima: Piemonte-Lombardia. 1934. pp.[ii].255. [750.]

    — Parte seconda: Veneto–Venezia Giulia-Venezia Tridentina. 1937. pp.3–193. [600.]

    — Parte terza: Emilia–Liguria. 1938. pp.206. [350.]

also issued by the Ministerio dell'educazione nazionale; no more published.

SIMONETTA NICOLINI, Bibliografia degli antichi cataloghi a stampa di biblioteche italiana (secoli XVII e XVIII). Contributi alla biblioteca bibliografica italica (no.5): Firenze 1954. pp.136. [123.]

GIOVANNI CECCHINI, Le biblioteche pubbliche degli enti locali. Sussidi eruditi (no.12): Roma 1957. pp.163. [1000.]

Netherlands

G[ERRIT] A[LBERT] EVERS, Nederlandsche bibliografie van boek- en bibliotheekwezen. Centrale vereeniging voor openbare leeszalen en bibliotheken: 's-Gravenhage [Utrecht].

   1910. pp.40. [900.]
   1911. pp.52. [1100.]

F[RIEDRICH] K[ARL] H[EINRICH] KOSSMANN, Nederlandsch bibliotheekleven, 1908–1940. Een overzicht van den inhoud der vaktijdschriften uitgegeven door de Centrale vereeniging voor openbare leeszalen en bibliotheken en de Nederlandsche vereeniging van bibliothecarissen. Uitgeversfonds der bibliotheekvereenigingen: 's-Gravenhage 1941. pp.xi.coll.80. [3000.]

Poland

BIBLIOGRAFIA bibliografii i nauki o książce. Pańtswowy instytut książki: Łodz. 1945 &c.
details of this work are entered under Poland.

Russia

O[SKAR] E[DVARDOVICH] VOLTSENBURG, Систематический указатель книг и статей на русском языке по вопросам библиотечной техники. Библиография библиотековедения (vol.i): Петроград 1923. pp.3-52. [179.]

N[IKOLAI] N[IKOLAEVICH] ORLOV, Библиография библиотековедения (1917-1927). Русское библиографическое общество при Московском университете (no.119): Москва &c. 1928. pp.176. [795.]
limited to russian writings.

RAISSA MAURIN, A survey of soviet literature in library science, 1948-1952. Catholic university of America: Department of library service: Washington 1954. ff.[i].ix.149. [413.]*

Spain

RUDOLF HOECKER, Das spanische bibliothekswesen. Versuch einer bibliotheco-bibliographie. Archiv für bibliographie, buch- u. bibliothekswesen (beiheft 2): Linz a. d. Donau 1928. pp.62. [663.]

CONCEPCÍO DE BALANZÓ, Les biblioteques populars de la generalitat de Catalunya. Notes bibliogràfiques per a llur història. Escola de bibliotecàries de la generalitat de Catalunya: Quaderns de treball (no.3): Barcelona 1935. pp.204. [1750.]

CARLOS RAMOS RUIZ, Catálogo de la documentación referente a los archivos, bibliotecas y museos arqueologicos, que se custodia en el archivo del Ministerio de educación nacional. Cuerpo facultativo de archiveros, bibliotecarios y arqueólogos: Madrid 1950. pp.xvi.451. [4000.]

Switzerland

J. H. GRAF, Bibliographische vorarbeiten der landeskundlichen litteratur und kataloge der bibliotheken der Schweiz. Centralkommission für schweizerische landeskunde: Bibliographie der schweizerischen landeskunde (section 1a): Bern 1894. pp.xvi.67. [800.]

United States

T. H. MCKEE, Reports of the Committee on the Library, House of representatives, from the fourteenth congress, 1815, to the forty-ninth congress, 1887, inclusive. Washington 1887. pp.7. [150.]

T. H. MCKEE, Reports of the Committee on the Library, United States Senate, from the organization of the committee, December 10, 1822, to the close of the forty-ninth congress, 1887. Washington 1887. pp.8. [150.]

HUGH WILLIAMS, College libraries in the United States. Contribution toward a bibliography. University of the state of New York: State library bulletin (bibliography no.19): Albany 1899. pp. 609–655. [500.]

LIST of references on research facilities in american libraries. Library of Congress: Washington 1916. ff.5. [47.]*

LIST of references on state libraries. Library of Congress: Washington 1916. ff.3. [38.]*

LIST of references on county libraries. Library of Congress: Washington 1923. ff.8. [103.]*
— [supplement]. 1932. ff.9. [115.]*

DOROTHY ALICE PLUM, A bibliography of american college library administration, 1899–1926. New York state library: Bibliography bulletin (no.77): Albany 1926. pp.3–83. [750.]

FRANCES N. BAKER [*and others*], References on school libraries, 1920–26. New York state library: Bibliography bulletin (no.78): Albany 1927. pp. 3–37. [450.]

JAMES G[OODWIN] HODGSON, Regional library cooperation in the Rocky mountain region and the northern great plain, 1935–1953. A bibliography. Bibliographic center for research: Bulletin (no.10): Denver 1954. pp.20. [246.]*

LIBRARIANSHIP in the United States. A bibliography. United States information service: Series of bibliographies in american studies: [Rome 1957]. pp.72. [650.]

HARRY BACH, Bibliographical essay on the history of scholarly libraries in the United States, 1800 to the present. University of Illinois: Library school: Occasional papers (no.54): Urbana 1959. pp.24. [134.]*

5. *Special types of libraries*

SELECT list of references on special libraries. Library of Congress: Washington 1912. ff.13. [156.]*

LIST of references on traveling libraries. Library of Congress: Washington 1916. ff.10. [134.]*

LIST of references on business libraries. Library of Congress: Washington 1917. ff.7. [69.]*

RAILROAD libraries. Library of Congress: Washington 1922. ff.2. [13.]*

GWENDOLEN REES, Libraries for children. A history and a bibliography. 1924. pp.260. [1750.]

LIST of books on school libraries (including for the greater part only more recent publications). Library of Congress: [Washington] 1924. ff.9. [70.]★

PRISON libraries. Russell Sage foundation: Library: Bulletin (no.99): New York 1930. pp.4. [50.]

NORA E[RNESTINE] BEUST, School library administration. An annotated bibliography. Office of education: Bulletin (1941, no.7): Washington 1941. pp.vi.82. [716.]

A[UGUSTUS] F[REDERICK] KUHLMAN, College and university library problems. Selected references. . . . Preliminary edition. Nashville, Tenn. 1942. ff.[iii].43. [600.]★

BIBLIOTHERAPY. A bibliography 1900–1952. Veterans administration: Medical and general reference library: Washington 1952. pp.[ii].18. [378.]★
— [another edition]. Bibliotherapy hospitals . . . 1900–1957. Compiled by Rosemary Dolan . . . June Donelly . . . June Mitchell. 1958. pp.[v].46. [264.]

[STOYAN SHIKLEV *and others*], Сто години народни читалища. Библиографски указател. Български библиографски институт Елин Пелин: Поредица библиографии (no.16): София 1956. pp.180. [1215.]

MARIETTA DANIELS, Bibliotecas infantiles y escolares. Una bibliografía. Unión panamericana: Departamento de asuntos culturales: Bibliographic series (no.45): Washington 1955. pp.iv.20. [309.]*

MARY ØRVIG, Barnen böckerna, barnbibliotekarien. Bibliografi. Bibliotekjänst: Lund 1963. pp. [iii].32. [750.]*

6. *Librarianship*

LIBRARY science. [Library of Congress: Catalog division: Washington 1910]. pp.4. [50.]
— [ninth edition]. [1935]. pp.4. [100.]

BOOKS and pamphlets on library work. [A.L.A. books and pamphlets]. American library association: Chicago [?1923]. &c.
in progress.

REGINALD G. WILLIAMS, Courses of study in library science. Bolton 1924. pp.112. [1000.]
— — 1926. pp.xii.200. [2000.]

UNION list of literature on library science and

bibliography up to 1935. League of young librarians: Ôsaka 1938. pp.260. [2375.]

[C. W. MORRIS], A list of books on librarianship and library technique of interest to school librarians. School library association: 1939. pp.20. [49.]

— — A list of general reference books suitable for secondary school libraries [*on cover:* Third edition] and a list of books on librarianship & library technique of interest to school librarians. [By Cecil Ainsworth Stott]. [*on cover:* Second edition]. Revised by C[harles] H[umphrey] C[aulfield] Osborne. 1950. pp.52. [libraries: 186.]

— — Fourth edition. . . . Third edition. 1954. pp.[ii].62. [381.]

EDUCATION for librarianship. Grants-in-aid financed by the Carnegie corporation of New York, 1929–1942. American library association: Committee on fellowships and scholarships: Chicago 1943. pp.[iii].113. [96.]

consists largely of a bio-bibliographical list of recipients.

JORGE AGUAYO, Lista de obras de bibliotecología y bibliografía existentes en la biblioteca general de la universidad. La Habana 1948. ff.[ii].19. [292.]*

TRAINING for librarianship. Library of Congress: Washington 1948. ff.3. [15.]*

BIBLIOGRAFÍA de bibliografías y biblioteconomía 1936–1948. Universidad nacional mayor de San Marcos: Biblioteca central: Lima 1949. pp.28. [369.]

H. CARLOS ARAÚJO, Bibliografía sobre bibliotecnia. Obras existentes en bibliotecas uruguayas. Montevideo 1952. pp.[iii].47. [816.]*

KHR[ISTO] TRENKOV, Какво да четем по библиотечно дело и библиография. Препоръчителна библиография. Български библиографски институт Елин Пелин: София 1955. pp.48. [259.]

A BIBLIOGRAPHY of librarianship, being a select list of books available to students in the library. North-western polytechnic: 1956. pp.24. [500.]

БИБЛИОГРАФИЯ библиотековедения. Аннотированный указатель. Государственная... библиотека СССР имени В. И. Ленина: Научно-методический кабинет библиотековедения: Москва.

1956. pp.99.83.94.112. [1707.]
1957. pp.115.107.112.116. [1966.]
[*continued as:*]

БИБЛИОТЕКОВЕДЕНИЕ и библиография. Указатель литературы.

1958. pp.119.104.119.140. [1944.]
1959. pp.135.132.123.142. [2500.]
1960. pp.130.133.112.122. [2500.]
in progress.

M. C. TAYLOR, A union list of publications on library science and related subjects held by municipal libraries of Bankstown, Burwood, Canterbury, Marrickville, Rockdale. Municipal library: Canterbury [N.Z.] 1957. ff.[ix].44. [384.]*

LIBRARIANSHIP and allied subjects. A catalogue of books and periodicals in the reference library of interest to students of librarianship. Public libraries [Ealing] 1957. pp.[iii].47. [450.]*
— 2nd cumulative supplement. [1959]. pp.[12]. [75.]*

D[AVID] J[AMES] BRYANT and R[OGER] J[ULIAN] CRUDGE, Union list of professional textbooks, books on librarianship and allied subjects in libraries in Gloucestershire, Somerset and Wiltshire. Association of assistant libraries: Bristol and district division: 1958. pp.[iv].57. [1100.]*

LA COLECCIÓN bibliotecológica. Instituto de intercambio cultural argentino-norteamericano: Córdoba 1958. ff.16. [50.]*

[V. V. NEUMANN and E. E. TROITSKAYA],

Книга молодежи. В помощь массовым библиотекам. Государственная ордена Ленина библиотека СССР имени В. И. Ленина: Научно-методический отдел библиотековедения и библиографии: Москва 1959. pp.220. [400.]

EMMA LINARES, Bibliografía bibliotecológica. Unión panamericana: Departamento de asuntos: Bibliographic series (no.49): Washington 1960. pp.ix.233. [2000.]

BÜCHER zum bibliothekswesen. Bestandsverzeichnis. Zentralinstitut für bibliothekswesen: Fachbibliothek: [Berlin 1960]. pp.186. [1600.]

THE LITERATURE of library technical services. A survey of the publications. University of Illinois: Library school: Occasional papers (no.58): Urbana 1960. pp.48. [250.]*
— Revised. 1963. pp.46. [250.]*

7. *Library buildings*

[LOUISE BEERSTECHER], A reading list on library buildings. Bulletin of bibliography pamphlets (no.5): Boston 1898. pp.15. [150.]

BRIEF list of references on library buildings, their design and construction. Library of Con-

gress: Washington 1922. ff.7. [87.]★
— Additional references. 1932. ff.4. [132.]★

RECENT books and periodical articles on library architecture. Library of Congress: Washington 1947. ff.22. [185.]★

8. *Miscellaneous*

JOHN CARSON RATHER and NATHAN M[ARSHALL] COHEN, Statistics of libraries. An annotated bibliography of recurring surveys. Office of education: [Washington 1961]. pp.v.50. [156.]★

EDWARD MACK MCCORMICK, Bibliography on mechanized library processes. National science foundation: Office of science information service: Washington 1963. ff.[i].27. [155.]★

Reference books.

JOSEPH A. HANSLIK, Geschichte und beschreibung der Prager universitätsbibliothek. Prag 1851. pp. [vi].634. [2000.]

half the book consists of a catalogue of the reading room.

— — Zusätze und inhalts-verzeichnisse . . . von I[gnác] J[an] Hanus. 1863. pp.viii.92. [180.]

A LIST of the books in the reading room of the British museum. [By William Brenchley Rye]. 1859. pp.xxxi.413. [7000.]

— Second edition. 1871. pp.xxviii.349. [7000.]

— Third edition. List of the books of reference [&c.]. [By Alfred William Pollard]. 1889. pp. xxvi.476. [6500.]

— Fourth edition. List of books forming the reference library [&c.]. [By R. F. Sharp, R. A. Streatfield and W. A. Marsden]. 1910. pp.xxviii. 1130+[ii].538. [25,000.]

СИСТЕМАТИЧЕСКІЙ каталогъ книгъ, находящихся въ читальной залѣ Императорской публичной библіотеки. Санктпетербургъ 1862. pp.[vi].71. [2000.]

Reference Books

PERIODICALS currently received; and works of reference in the Reading room and at the desk in Bates hall. Public library: Boston 1870. pp.31. [reference: 350.]

CATALOGUE alphabétique des ouvrages mis à la libre disposition des lecteurs dans la salle de travail. Bibliothèque nationale: 1879. pp.xx.257. [2000.]
— — 4ᵉ édition. Catalogue alphabétique des livres imprimés mis à la disposition des lecteurs dans la salle de travail, suivi de la liste des catalogues usuels du Département des manuscrits. 1933. pp. 3–142. [3000.]
there are several intermediate editions.

BOOKS for a reference library. Being lectures on the books in the Reference department of the Free public library, Birmingham. First series. 1885. pp.192. [2000.]

HENRY TENNYSON FOLKARD, Bibliography in the Reference department of the Wigan free public library. Wigan 1887. pp.[ii].56. [1750.]
12 copies privately printed.

A[DOLF] GROWOLL, A bookseller's library. New York 1891. pp.[vii].72. [400.]

VERZEICHNIS der lesesaal- und handbibliothek.

Universitäts-bibliothek: Berlin 1891. pp.vii.132. [1232.]

— Fünfte ausgabe. [By Edmund Georg Schneider and Victor Loewe]. 1906. pp.viii.251. [2364.]

— — Nachtrag. [By E. G. Schneider]. 1912. pp.[iv].76. [800.]

[JOSÉ MARIA VIGIL], Catálogos de la Biblioteca nacional de México. Primera división. Introducción a los primeros conocimientos humanos. México 1894. pp.81. [1500.]

[FRIEDRICH CLEMENS EBRARD], Verzeichniss der handbibliothek des lesesaals. Stadtbibliothek: Frankfurt a. M. 1894. pp.iv.50. [750.]

— Fünfte auflage. [By — Traut]. 1913. pp. [iv].232. [3000.]

VERZEICHNISS der handbibliothek des Lesesaales der Universitäts-bibliothek zu Leipzig. 1896. pp. viii.140. [1750.]

— Dritte ausgabe. 1905. pp.viii.198. [2000.]

REFERENCE catalogue of the Reynolds library. Rochester, N.Y. 1898. pp.x.324. [8000.]

SELECTION of reference books for use of cataloguers in finding full names. [New York] State library: Bulletin: Bibliography (no.5): Albany 1898. pp.98–114. [250.]

— [second edition]. A selection of cataloguers reference books . . . (no.84 = Bibliography no.36): 1903. pp.235–416. [750.]

largely printed on one side of the leaf.

EDWARD M. BORRAJO, Books for the reference library. Some selected lists, and a suggestion. 1899. pp.11. [175.]

privately printed.

A LIST of books in the Reading room. John Crerar library: Chicago 1900. pp.251. [2000.]

— [second edition]. 1909. pp.viii.488. [3500.]

ALICE BERTHA KROEGER, Guide to the study and use of reference books. American library association: A.L.A. annotated lists: Boston &c. 1902. pp.viii.106. [1250.]

— — Seventh edition. Guide to reference books. By Constance M[abel] Winchell. Chicago 1951. pp.xvii.645. [6000.]

the intermediate editions are by Isadore Gilbert Mudge.

— — — Supplement.

    i. 1950–1952. pp.[vii].117. [800.]
    ii. 1953–1955. pp.[vii].134. [1000.]
    iii. 1954–1958.
    iv. 1959–1962. pp.vii.151. [1000.]

Reference Books

WILHELM HAAS, Katalog der handbibliotheken des katalogzimmers und lesesaales der K.k. universitäts-bibliothek. Wien 1904. pp.[iv].384. [25,000.]

—— 2. ausgabe. 1908. pp.[iv].447. [30,000.]

——— I. nachtrag. 1910. pp.40. [1000.]

——— II. nachtrag. 1912. pp.39. [1000.]

ARNIM GRAESEL, Führer für bibliotheksbenutzer. Leipzig 1905. pp.viii.102. [600.]

—— Zweite . . . auflage. 1913. pp.xii.266. [2500.]

VERZEICHNIS der im lesezimmer aufgestellten handbibliothek. Stadtbibliothek: Danzig 1906. pp.[vi].52. [1000.]

PITMAN's where to look. An easy guide to books of reference. 1907. pp.xvii.151. [300.]

— Fourth edition. 1911. pp.xviii.134. [500.]

SUBJECT list of works of reference, biography, the auxiliary historical sciences, etc., in the library of the Patent office. Patent office library: Subject lists (n.s. AA–BE): 1908. pp.336. [2000.]

VERZEICHNIS der im grossen lesesaale aufgestellten handbibliothek. Vierte ausgabe. Königliche bibliothek: Berlin 1909. pp.xiii.263. [3000.]

I. V. VLADISLAVSKEV [*pseud.* IGNATY VLADIS-

ʟᴀᴠᴏᴠɪᴄʜ ɢᴏʟʙɪɴsᴋʏ], Что читать ? Указатель
систематическаго домашняго чтенія для
учашихся. Москва 1911. pp.56. [500.]

ᴄᴀᴛᴀʟᴏɢᴜᴇ des ouvrages mis à la libre disposition des lecteurs dans la salle de lecture de la
section des imprimés. Bibliothèque royale:
Bruxelles 1923. pp.xiv.97. [63.]

[ғʀᴀɴᴢ ᴋᴏᴄʜ], Verzeichnis der handbibliothek
des Druckschriften-lesesaales der Nationalbibliothek. Wien 1923. pp.viii.295. [4000.]
—— ɪ. nachtrag. 1924. pp.20. [200.]
—— ɪɪ. nachtrag. 1925. pp.19. [200.]
—— ɪɪɪ. nachtrag. 1926. pp.17. [175.]
—— ɪᴠ. nachtrag. 1927. pp.18. [175.]

ᴊóᴢᴇғ ɢʀʏᴄᴢ, Katalog bibljoteki podręcznej
czytelni oraz biura katalogowego. Bibljoteka
jagiellońska: Kraków 1925. pp.xii.219. [3000.]

ʟɪsᴛ of books in class 'Ref' (Cockerell's build-
ing). University library: Cambridge 1927. pp.
[iii].106. [1000.]

ᴢᴀɪᴅᴇᴇ ᴍᴀʙᴇʟ ʙʀᴏᴡɴ, The library key. 1928.
—— [another edition]. The new library key.
By Margaret G[erry] Cook. 1956. pp.viii.136.
[500.]

Reference Books

GÖTTINGER handkatalog. Lesesaalbibliothek. Bibliographischer apparat und handmagazin der Universitätsbibliothek. Göttingen 1929. pp.xvi. 636. [10,000.]

JOHN MINTO, Reference books. A classified and annotated guide to the principal works of reference. Library association: 1929. pp.vii.356. [5000.]
—— Supplement. 1931. pp.vii.140. [1750.]

ARNE V. FRANDSEN, Haandbogsfortegnelse. Vejledning ved kjøb og benyttelse af de vigtigste haandbøger. Danmarks biblioteksforenings skrifter (vol.ii): København 1930. pp.[vii].131. [500.]

A SELECT list of annuals . . . and books of reference . . . in the Reference department. Municipal libraries: Bath [1930]. pp.17. [450.]
— [another edition]. [1936]. pp.22. [600.]

CATÁLOGO de los libros de la Sala general. Bibliotheca nacional: Madrid 1931. pp.viii.427. [9000.]

B. M. HEADICAR, Aids to research. . . . With select bibliographies of reference books, bibliographical guides and specialist dictionaries, by C. Fuller. 1931. pp.9–16. [70.]

KAREL HOCH, Tisíc knih pro bibliothekáře.

Reference Books

Veř[ejná] a univ[ersitní] knihovna: Příručky pro vědecké knihovny (vol.i): Praze 1932. pp.192. [1100.]

ROBERT W. DESMOND, Newspaper reference methods. Minneapolis 1933. pp.xv.229. [1250.]

HAANDBOGSKATALOG, Fortegnelse over Hovedbibliotekets haandbogsamling af dansk og udenlandsk litteratur. Kommunebiblioteker: København 1935. pp.viii.108. [2000.]

SSŬ-YÜ TÊNG and KNIGHT BIGGERSTAFF, An annotated bibliography of selected chinese reference works. Yenching journal of chinese studies: Monograph (no.12): Peiping 1936. pp.vi.271. [300.]
—— Revised edition. Harvard-Yenching institute studies (vol.xii): Cambridge, Mass. 1951. pp.x.326. [400.]

P. M. SPEIGHT, Reference books for the small library. South African library association: South african libraries: Reprint (no.2): Pretoria 1935. pp.12. [75.]

AAGE BREDSTED [and others], 500 haandbøger. Udvalg of nyere haandbogsliteratur. Aarhus 1936. pp.48. [500.]

Reference Books

RUBY ETHEL CUNDIFF, Recommended reference books for the high school library. Chicago 1936. pp.16. [100.]

—— Fifth edition. Nashville 1955. pp.28. [200.]

ANTHONY G. HEPBURN, Writers' guide to information. Writers' & artists' library: 1937. pp.vii. 151. [1000.]

CATALOGUE of the code books, dictionaries, directories, maps, periodicals that may be consulted at the Southwark commercial library. Southwark public libraries and museum committee: 1937. pp.79. [500.]

HAROLD G. RUSSELL, THOMAS P. FLEMING and BLANCHE MOEN, The use of books and libraries. . . . Fourth edition. University of Minnesota: Minneapolis 1937. pp.v.79. [500.]

—— Eighth edition. By H. G. Russell, Raymond H. Shove and B. E. Moen. 1955. pp.v.93. [250.]

the earlier editions, 1933–1936, were not printed.

W[ILLIA]M A[LFRED] BAGLEY, Facts and how to find them. A guide to the sources of information. 1937. pp.101. [500.]

—— Fifth [*sic*] edition. [1958]. pp.135. [750.]

Reference Books

J. D. COWLEY, The use of reference material. 1937. pp.158. [200.]

MARY NEILL BARTON, A guide to reference books. Enoch Pratt free library: Baltimore 1938. pp.44. [375.]

— — Fourth edition. Reference books. 1959. pp.117. [400.]
this is the fourth edition under the new title.

LOUIS SHORES, Basic reference books. An introduction to the evaluation, study, and use of reference materials. . . . Second edition. American library association: Chicago 1939. pp.xiii.472. [300.]
— — [another edition]. Basic reference sources. . . . With a chapter on science reference sources by Helen Focke. 1954. pp.ix.378. [1000.]

[C. W. MORRIS], A list of books on librarianship . . . and a list of general reference books. School library association: 1939. pp.20. [reference: 57.]
— — A list of general reference books suitable for secondary school libraries [*on cover:* Third edition] and a list of books on librarianship & library technique of interest to school librarians. [By Cecil Ainsworth Stott]. [*on cover:* Second edition]. Revised by C[harles] H[umphrey]

C[aulfield] Osborne. 1950. pp.52. [reference: 102.]
— — Fourth edition. . . . Third edition. 1954.
pp.[ii].62. [381.]

THE CLASSIFIED list of reference books and periodicals for college libraries. Southern association of colleges and secondary schools: Commission on colleges and universities: Atlanta 1940. pp.40. [250.]
— — Third edition. W[illiam] Stanley Hoole, editor. 1955. pp.xi.227. [reference: 1447.]

AMALIA VAGO, La sala di consultazione. Enciclopedia del libro: Milano [1941]. pp.5–209.

W[ILLIAM] A[RTHUR] MUNFORD, Reference books. Second edition. National book council: Book list (no.158): 1942. pp.6. [180.]

HERBERT S[IMON] HIRSHBERG, Subject guide to reference books. American library association: Chicago 1942. pp.xvi.260. [3000.]

ZAIDEE [MABEL] BROWN, Short cuts to information. New York 1943. pp.[ii].97–124. [400.]

SUGGESTED list of books for the library of the United Nations conference on international organization, San Francisco, 1945. Library of Congress: Washington 1945. ff.131. [1330.]*

— [supplement]. 1945. ff.22. [200.]★
— — 1945. ff.8. [70.]★

A LIST of the government publications and other pamphlets and the atlases, directories, gazetteers, newspapers and magazines and year books in the reference department of the Central public library. [Gateshead] 1946. pp.38. [1000.]

OLGA PINTO, Guida bibliografica per lo studente di lettere e di magistero. Roma 1947. pp.3–134. [360.]

REFERENCE books: a select list. Library of Congress: Washington 1948. ff.12. [112.]★

A[RTHUR] D[ENIS] ROBERTS, Introduction to reference books. Library association: 1948. pp. viii.181. [250.]
— — Third edition. [1956]. pp.ii.237. [400.]

RUBY ETHEL CUNDIFF, Recommended reference books for the elementary school library. Chicago &c. 1949. pp.[ii].33. [228.]
— — [second edition]. [1951]. pp.[ii].35. [250.]

GERTRUD SAVELSBERG, Internationales informationsmaterial. Bibliothek des Instituts für weltwirtschaft: Kiel 1950. pp.[iv].19. [150.]★

L. N[OËLLE] MALCLÈS, Les sources du travail

bibliographique. Genève &c. 1950–1958. pp.xvi.
364+[ii].ix.954+x.572. [20,000.]

L[EONARD] M[ASLIN] PAYNE and E[DWARD]
P[ERRY] DUDLEY, A select list of reference books
and bibliographies for the use of students preparing for . . . examinations of the Library association. [Second edition]. North-western polytechnic: Department of librarianship: 1951. pp.50.
[561.]

LIONEL R[OY] MCCOLVIN and R[OBERT] L[EWIS]
W[RIGHT] COLLISON, Reference library stock. An
informal guide. 1952. pp.vii.312. [4000.]

NEW reference books. Additions to the reference collections (other than continuations) in the
main reading room, the Thomas Jefferson reading
room, the Study room reference and the General
reference and bibliography division. Library of
Congress: Washington April 1951–May 1952.
ff.[297]. [2765.]

JAVIER LASSO DE LA VEGA, *ed.* Catálogo abreviado
de una selección de libros de consulta, referencía,
estudio y enseñanza. Junta de intercambio y
adquisición de libros para bibliotecas publicas:
Madrid 1953. pp.xxiv.931. [11,279.]

KHWAJA NUR ELAHI, A. MOID and AKHTAR H.

SIDDIQUI, A guide to works of reference published in Pakistan. Pakistan bibliographical working group: Publication (no.1): [Karachi] 1953. pp.36. [350.]

A[LBERT] J[OHN] WALFORD, Union list of reference books . . . in some metropolitan & greater London libraries. Association of assistant libraries: Greater London division: 1954. pp.76. [400.]

P. K. GARDE, Directory of reference works published in Asia. Unesco bibliographical handbooks (no.5): Paris 1956. pp.xxix.139. [1619.]

JOSEFA EMILIA SABOR, Manual de fuentes de información. Obras de referencia. Contribuciones bibliotecológicas (no.2): Buenos Aires [1957]. pp. xiv.337. [1200.]

JOSEFA EMILIA SABOR, Manual de fuentes de información. Buenos Aires [1957]. pp.xiv.337. [2000.]

JOHN HIRST, First steps in reference work. A handbook for students. Sydney 1957. pp.[ii].iv.39. [50.]

ROBERT W. MURPHEY, How and where to look it up? A guide to standard sources of information. New York &c. [1958]. pp.xiv.721. [5000.]

Reference Books

G[ILBERT] R. MORRIS, Reference books for public libraries. South african library association: Johannesburg 1958. ff.36. [300.]*

A[LBERT] J[OHN] WALFORD and L[EONARD] M[ASLIN] PAYNE, Guide to reference material. Library association: 1959. pp.viii.543. [4500.]

LIONEL STEBBING, Where to find the facts. [1959]. pp.3-66. [750.]*

BASIC reference books for Georgia public libraries. Division of instructional materials and library services: [Atlanta] 1959. pp.[ii].27. [350.]*

[CHARLES A. TOASE and BRIAN C. SKILLING], Reference books for the home. Public libraries: Wimbledon 1959. pp.19. [150.]*

[AXEL ANDERSEN and TORBEN NIELSEN], Håndbogsfortegnelse. Danmarks biblioteksskole: København 1962. ff.164. [750.]*

ALAN PULLEN, Words of persuasion. Reference books for retarded readers. Birmingham [1962]. pp.128. [150.]

ELIZABETH H. HALL, Handbooks. Armed services technical information agency: Arlington, Va. 1962. pp.vi.124.

JÁNOS SZENTMIHÁLYI and MIKLÓS VÉRTESY, *edd.*

Útmutató a tudományos munka magyar és nemzetközi irodalmához. Budapest 1963. pp.732. [10,000.]

WILLIAM SUNNERS, How and where to find the facts. Arco reference library: New York [1963]. pp.ix.442. [5000.]

A[LEX] SANDRI WHITE, Fact-finding made easy. A new guide to informational sources. Central Valley, N.Y. 1963. ff.137. [2000.]*

CHOIX d'usuels proposé aux bibliothèques municipales. Direction des bibliothèques de France: 1963. pp.[iii].172. [851.]*

UNION list of expensive, out-of-print and specialized reference books in libraries in Orange county. Second edition. Orange county library association: [s.l.] 1963. ff.v.185.*

G[EORGE] CHANDLER, How to find out. A guide to sources of information for all. Oxford &c. [1963]. pp.xiii.185. [750.]

REFERENCE books. Pacific air forces: PACAF basic bibliographies: [San Francisco] 1963. pp.[ii]. viii.181. [450.]*

Reference Books

VIRGINIA A[SHWORTH] STERNBERG, How to
locate technical information. Complete manage-
ment library (vol.xxviii): Waterford, Conn.
[1964]. pp.viii.111. [500.]

Blind, books for the.

[only a few specimens have been set out of the numerous catalogues of books reproduced for the blind.]

1. Periodicals, 174.
2. General, 175.
3. Music, 180.
4. Miscellaneous, 180.

1. *Periodicals*

IDA HIRST-GIFFORD and RUTH E. WILCOX, Compilation of Braille periodicals and inkprint magazines relating to the blind in the United States and abroad. 1929. pp.35. [140.]

—— Third edition. Directory of periodicals of special interest to the blind. Compiled by Helga Lende. American foundation for the blind: New York 1938. pp.[v].66. [271.]*

PERIODICALS of special interest to blind persons in Canada and the United States. American foundation for the Blind: New York 1956. pp.36. [150.]

— [another edition]. 1960. pp.38.3. [150.]*

Books for the Blind

2. General

CATALOGUS van de Nederlandsche blinden-bibliotheek. 's-Gravenhage 1902. pp.53. [1500.]

KATALOG der blindenbibliothek im K. K. blin-den-erziehungsinstitut in Wien. Wien 1904. pp. 45. [800.]

FINDING list of books for the blind deposited in the Public library of Cincinnati by the Cincinnati library society for the blind. Cincinnati 1905. pp. 20. [750.]

LIST of books in the library for the blind. New York state library: Bibliography (no.55): Albany 1915. pp.5-116. [2500.]
— Supplement . . . (no.63): 1919. pp.5-68. [1506.]
— Supplement . . . (no.68): 1922. pp.5-67. [1250.]

CATALOGUE général des ouvrages imprimés pour les aveugles en France et en Suisse romande. Société d'impression et de reliure du livre pour les aveugles: 1920. pp.32. [930.]

A LIST of braille books in the Department for the blind. Public library: St. Louis [c.1920]. pp.[15]. [1400.]

NEW YORK point books in the Room for the blind. Library of Congress: Washington 1921. pp.37. [1000.]

MOON type books in the room for the blind. Library of Congress: Washington 1921. pp.16. [400.]

LIST of books in New York point and revised braille at the Minnesota school for the blind: [Faribault] 1924. pp.35. [800.]

BRAILLE grade one and a half books. Library of Congress: Room [*afterwards:* Service] for the blind: Washington 1925. pp.[ii].38. [1000.]
— [third edition]. Catalogue of publications in braille-grade 1½. 1930. pp.iv.86. [3000.]

UNION catalogue of hand-copied material in braille-grade 1½ in the Library of Congress and various other libraries useful to students and advanced readers. Washington 1931. pp.iv.33. [750.]

CATALOGO. Biblioteca nazionale dei ciechi 'Regina Margherita'. Genova [1931]. pp.34. [750.]

CATALOG of the library in braille, grades 1, 1½ and 2. Minnesota school for the blind: [Faribault] 1932. pp.36. [1500.]

LIST of books selected. Library of Congress:

Project, books-for-the blind: Washington 1932. pp.[6]. [150.]

BRAILLE book review. American foundation for the blind. New York 1932 &c.

in progress.

CATALOGUE of books. National library for the blind: 1937. pp.335. [20,000.]

BOOKS for children with seriously defective vision. Albany 1939. pp.15. [200.]

TALKING books for the blind. Catalog of titles placed in the distributing libraries August 1934 to June 1938. Library of Congress: Project, books for the adult blind: Washington 1939. pp.16. [300.]

— [another edition]. Catalog of talking books for the blind, 1934–1948. Library of Congress: Division for the blind: 1949. pp.x.188. [1500.]

— — Supplement no.1, 1948–1950. pp.xii.28. [200.]

— — 1953–1957. pp.xvi.145. [1000.]

BOOKS in braille 1931–1938. Catalog of titles placed in the distributing libraries. Library of Congress: Project, books for the adult blind; Washington 1939. pp.viii.95. [1078.]

— [another edition]. Catalog of press braille books provided by the Library of Congress, 1931–

1948. Library of Congress: Division for the blind: 1950. pp.ix.163. [2000.]

— — Cumulative supplement, 1948–54. pp.xii. 59. [1000.]

RENÉ LABBÉ [*and others*], Catalogue des livres de la bibliothèque des aveugles. Bibliothèque municipale: [Blois 1942]. pp.ii.26. [600.]

SAVE your eyes. A list of library books for visually handicapped children, grades 1–8, recommended by the Oregon state department of education and the Oregon state library. [Salem 1947]. pp.[i].22. [200.]★

LORRAINE GALISDORFER, A new annotated reading guide for children with partial vision. Buffalo [1950]. pp.94. [600.]

CATALOGUE of books. National library for the blind: 1950–1952. pp.158–293. [20,000.]

CHARLOTTE MATSON and LOLA LARSON, Books for tired eyes. A list of books in large print. Fourth edition. American library association: Chicago 1951. pp.[vii].77. [1600.]

LIST of books in New York point at the Minnesota school for the blind. [Faribault] 1951. pp.25. [500.]

CATALOGUE of books in moon type. National library for the blind: 1952. pp.24. [1000.]

UNION CATALOG of hand-copied books in braille. Library of Congress: Division for the blind: Washington 1955. pp.viii.581. [15,000.]
— Supplement. 1960. pp.xii.105. [4200.]

CATALOGUE de la Bibliothèque Braille, intégral. Union des aveugles de guerre: 1957. pp.22. [400.]
— Catalogue . . . abrègé [sic] et amplifié. 1957. pp.30. [600.]

CATALOGUE of braille books, braille and letter-press periodicals and letterpress books. Royal national institute for the blind: 1957. pp.viii.222. [2000.]
— Supplement.
   i. 1959. pp.22. [250.]
   ii. 1960. pp.18. [200.]
   iii. 1961. pp.19. [200.]

BRAILLE books for juvenile readers. A cumulative list of titles issued since January 1, 1953. Library of Congress: Division for the blind: Washington 1958. pp.24. [200.]*
— [another edition]. 1960. pp.[iii].39. [400.]*

TALKING books for juvenile readers. A cumulative list of titles issued since January 1, 1953. Library of Congress: Division for the blind: Washington 1959. pp.[iii].35. [250.]*

CATALOG of recorded books. Recording for the blind: New York 1962. pp.[ii].141. [4000.]

BOOKS on magnetic tape. A catalog of tape recordings. Library of Congress: Division for the blind: [Washington] 1962. pp.x.127. [750.]*

3. *Music*

LIST of music for the blind . . . in the circulating department of the New York public library. [New York 1906]. pp.7. [350.]

CATALOGUE de musique éditée en braille à l'usage des aveugles. Société d'impression et de reliure du livre pour les aveugles: 1921. pp.51. [1500.]

4. *Miscellaneous*

MARCIA [MAY] HILL and DORA CROUTER, Save your eyes. A list of library books for visually handicapped children. Department of education: Division of special education: [Salem, Or. 1950]. pp.27. [175.]

READING for profit. An annotated list of press braille and talking books on vocational training, personal adjustment and economic advancement.

Library of Congress: Division for the blind: Washington 1960. pp.16. [142.]*
— Revised edition. 1963. pp.iii.29. [200.]*

BROADENING professional horizons. Selected readings in social welfare and related fields: currently available in Braille or recorded form. American foundation for the blind: New York 1961. pp.[ii].21. [150.]*

DONALD F. JOYCE, The Civil war. A list of . . . books in braille and on talking book records. Library of Congress: Division for the blind: Washington 1961. pp.7. [100.]

COUNSELING and rehabilitation. A list of books recorded on magnetic tape solely for the care of blind persons. Library of Congress: Division for the blind: Washington 1962. pp.[iii].10. [50.]*

Paleography.

1. *Bibliographies*

GIUSEPPE VALENTINELLI, Dei cataloghi a stampa di codici manoscritti. Venezia 1871. pp.152. [258.]

F. RULLMANN, Ueber die herstellung eines gedruckten generalkataloges der grossen manuscriptenschätze im Deutschen reiche. Bibliothekswissenschaftliches (vol.ii): Freiburg i. Br. 1875. pp.62. [100.]

consists in large part of a list of manuscript catalogues of german libraries.

ULYSSE ROBERT, État des catalogues des manuscrits des bibliothèques de France. 1877. pp.31. [150.]

125 copies printed.

ULYSSE ROBERT, État des catalogues des manuscrits des bibliothèques de Belgique et de Hollande. 1878. pp.x.26. [150.]

300 copies printed.

Palaeography

PAUL FAIDER, Bibliographie des catalogues des manuscrits des bibliothèques de Belgique. Bruges 1933. pp.16. [120.]

ERNEST CUSHING RICHARDSON, A union world catalog of manuscript books. . . . III. A list of printed catalogs of manuscript books. New York 1935. pp.v.386. [7000.]

GIUSEPPE GABRIELI, Notizie statistiche, storiche, bibliografiche delle collezioni di manoscritti oggi conservati nelle biblioteche italiane. Enciclopedia del libro: Milano 1936. pp.[iv].229. [2000.]

2. General

FRIEDERICH AUGUST HUCH, Versuch einer litteratur der diplomatik. Erlangen 1792. pp.xxii.151 +153–492. [1000.]

PETER [IVANOVICH] KEPPEN, Списокъ русскимъ памятникамъ, служащимъ къ составленію исторіи художествъ и отечественной палеографіи. Москва 1822. pp.k.viii.120. [174.]

[AUGUST] HEINRICH HOFFMANN [VON FALLERS-LEBEN], Handschriftenkunde für Deutschland. Breslau 1831. pp.48. [150.]

GEORGE STEPHENS, Förteckning öfver de förnämsta brittiska och fransyska handskrifterna, uti

Kongl. bibliotheket i Stockholm. Stockholm 1847. pp.xii.205. [50.]

[SIR J. THOMAS GILBERT], National manuscripts of Ireland. Account of facsimiles of national manuscripts of Ireland, from the earliest extant specimens to A.D. 1719 . . . selected and edited by John T. Gilbert. 1884. pp.[iii].356.lxxi. [400.]

LÉOPOLD [VICTOR] DELISLE, Mémoire sur l'école calligraphique de Tours au IXe siècle. 1885. pp.32. [25.]

CATALOGO delle opere di paleografia e diplomatica possedute dalla Biblioteca nazionale centrale Vittorio Emanuele di Roma. Roma [printed] 1887. coll.60. [200.]

[EDWARD WILLIAMS BYRON NICHOLSON], A brief conspectus of the cases in the Bodleian arranged to illustrate the history of latin and west european book-hands. By the Librarian. [Oxford] 1890. pp.[8]. [100.]

a copy containing ms. notes is in the Bodleian library.

[HENRI AUGUSTE OMONT], Liste des catalogues et livres imprimés mis à la disposition des lecteurs dans la salle de travail. Bibliothèque nationale: Département des manuscrits: 1891. pp.47. [920.]

reproduced from handwriting.

— — 4ᵉ édition. Catalogue alphabétique des livres [&c.] . . . suivi de la liste des catalogues usuels du Département. 1933. pp.142. [6000.]

HEINRICH NENTWIG, Die mittelalterlichen handschriften in der stadtbibliothek zu Braunschweig. Wolfenbüttel 1893. pp.vii.202. [2750.]

H[ENRI AUGUSTE] OMONT, Listes des recueils de facsimilés et des reproductions de manuscrits conservés à la Bibliothèque nationale. 1903. pp.[iii].69. [373.]

— — Deuxième édition. 1912. pp.[iii].291. [700.]

WORKS upon the study of greek and latin palæography and diplomatic in the John Rylands library. Manchester [1904]. pp.15. [200.]

INVENTARIO dell'antica biblioteca del s. convento di s. Francesco in Assisi, compilato nel 1381. Pubblicato . . . dal . . . Leto Alessandri. Società internazionale degli studi francescani: Assisi 1906. pp.xlvii.270. [500.]

MARGARET F. MOORE, Two select bibliographies of mediæval historical study. I. A classified list of works relating to the study of english palæography and diplomatic. . . . London school of economics: Studies in economics (Bibliographies, no.2): 1912. pp.25–70. [428.]

HUBERT NÉLIS, L'écriture et les scribes. [Répertoires des ouvrages à consulter:] Bruxelles 1918. pp.xii.159. [1544.]

JOHN WILKS and ARTHUR DOUGLAS LACEY, Catalogue of works dealing with the study of western palæography in the libraries of the university of London. 1921. pp.vi.106. [860.]

A LIST of references on the repair and restoration of manuscripts and documents. Library of Congress: [Washington] 1924. ff.5. [39.]*

ANTÓNIO ANSELMO, Os códices alcobacenses da Biblioteca nacional. I. Codices portugueses. Lisboa 1926. pp.80. [40.]

EDWARD KENNARD RAND, A survey of the manuscripts of Tours. Mediaeval academy of America: Publications (no.3): Cambridge, Mass. 1929–1934. pp.xxi.245+xvii.137. [250.]

MILKO KOS and FRANCE STELÈ, Srednjeveški rokopisi v Sloveniji. Umetnostno-Zgodovinsko društvo: Ljubljani 1931. pp.ix.247. [1000.]

AGUSTÍN MILLARES CARLO, Contribución al 'corpus' de códices visigóticos. Publicaciones de la Facultad de filosofía y letras, Universidad de Madrid (vol.i): Madrid 1931. pp.283. [100.]

PAUL SATTLER and GÖTZ VON SELLE, Bibliographie zur geschichte der schrift bis in das jahr 1930. Archiv für bibliographie (beiheft 17): Linz a. D. 1935. pp.xx.234. [3010.]

SEYMOUR [MONTEFIORE ROBERT ROSSO] DE RICCI and W[ILLIAM] J[EROME] WILSON, Census of medieval and renaissance manuscripts in the United States and Canada. American council of learned societies: New York 1935–1940. pp.iii–xxiii.1098 +iii–xviii.1103–2343+vii.222. [10,000.]
covers the period to 1600.

BERNHARD BISCHOFF, Die südostdeutschen schreibschulen und bibliotheken in der Karolingerzeit. Wiesbaden 1940 &c.
    i. Die bayrischen diözesen. 1960. pp.viii.280. [800.]
in progress.

GIOVANNI MUZZIOLI, Collezioni paleografiche dell'Istituto di paleografia. Catalogo. R. università: Roma 1943. pp.iii–xxxi.215. [2200.]
300 copies printed.

CODICUM in finibus Belgarum ante annum 1550 conscriptorum qui in bibliotheca universitatis asservantur. Bibliotheca universitatis Leidensis: Codices manuscripti (vol.v &c.): Lugduni Batavorum.

   i. Codices 168–360 societatis cui nomen Maatschappij der nederlandsche letterkunde descripsit G. I. Lieftinck ... (vol.v): 1948. pp.xxii.236. [2000.]

CATERINA SANTORO, Codices trivultiani antiquiores (ab VIII usque ad XII saeculum). Milano 1950. pp.3–57. [11.]
300 copies printed.

BERNHARD BISCHOFF and JOSEF HOFMANN, Libri sancti Kyliani. Die würzburger schreibschule und die dombibliothek im VIII. und IX. jahrhundert. Quellen und forschungen zur geschichte des bistums und hochstifts Würzburg (vol.vi): Würzburg 1952. pp.xi.200. [150.]

GUIDE to the irish manuscripts exhibited in the library of Trinity college, Dublin, on the occasion of xx xxxxxx. [Dublin] 1953. pp.28. [26.]

CATALOGUE des manuscrits en écriture latine portant des indications de date, de lieu ou de copiste. Par [or rather, edited by] Charles Samaran et Robert Marichal.

Palaeography

i. Monique Garand, Josette Metman and Marie Thérèse Vernet, Musée Condé et bibliothèques parisiennes. 1959. pp.xix. 496.[xi]+vol. of plates. [287.]

in progress.

KARL FORSTNER, Die karolingischen handschriften und fragmente in den salzburger bibliotheken (ende des 8. jh. bis ende des 9. jh.). Gesellschaft für salzburger landeskunde: Mitteilungen (suppl. vol.3): Salzburg 1962. pp.70. [56.]

AGUSTÍN MILLARES CARLO, Manuscritos visigóticos. Notas bibliográficas. Monumenta Hispaniæ sacra: Subsidia (vol.i): Barcelona &c. 1963. pp. [iv].108. [241.]

PAUL OSKAR KRISTELLER, Iter italicum. A finding list of uncatalogued or incompletely catalogued humanistic manuscripts of the renaissance in italian and other libraries. Warburg institute: 1963– . pp.xxviii.533+

in progress.

Papyri.

[JEAN FRANÇOIS CHAMPOLLION, *the younger*], Catalogo de' papiri egiziani della biblioteca Vaticana. [Translated by Angelo Mai]. Roma 1825. pp.viii.79. [35.]

[—] — Die aegyptischen papyrus der Vaticanischen bibliothek. Aus dem italienischen des Angelo Mai [or rather, from his translation] von Ludwig Bachmann. Leipzig 1827. pp.vi.30. [35.]

[JOSIAH FORSHALL], Description of the greek papyri in the British museum. Part I. 1839. pp. [iii].84. [44.]
no more published.

EDWARD HINCKS, Catalogue of the egyptian manuscripts in the library of Trinity college. Dublin 1843. pp.[ii].32. [19.]

THÉODULE DEVÉRIA, Catalogue des manuscrits égyptiens écrits sur papyrus, toile, tablettes et ostraca . . . qui sont conservés au Musée égyptien du Louvre. 1881. pp.[iv].272. [1000.]

WALTER SCOTT, Fragmenta herculanensia. A descriptive catalogue of the Oxford copies of the herculanean rolls. Oxford 1885. pp.xii.327.xli. [500.]

HORATIUS [ORAZIO] MARUCCHI, Monumenta papyracea bibliothecae Vaticanae. Romae 1891. pp.ix.137. [138.]

HORATIUS [ORAZIO] MARUCCHI, Monumenta papyracea latina bibliothecae Vaticanae. Romae 1895. pp.xi.57. [24.]

[HENRI AUGUSTE OMONT], Bulles pontificales sur papyrus (IXe–XIe siècle). Nogent-le-Rotrou [printed] 1904. pp.8. [23.]

ARTHUR S. HUNT [vol.ii: JOHN DE M. JOHNSON, VICTOR MARTIN and A. S. HUNT; iii: C. H. ROBERTS], Catalogue of the greek [vol.iii: and latin] papyri in the John Rylands library. Manchester 1911–1938. pp.xii.202+xx.487+xvii.217. [551.]

GUIDE to a special exhibition of greek and latin papyri presented . . . by the Egypt exploration fund. British museum: 1922. pp.20. [51.]

GERMAINE ROUILLARD, Les papyrus grecs de Vienne. Inventaire des documents publiés. 1923. pp.[iii].92. [1000.]

H. J. M. MILNE, Catalogue of the literary papyri in the British museum. 1927. pp.xvi.244. [257.]

Papyri

OLAF HANSEN, Die mittelpersischen papyri der papyrussammlung der staatlichen museen zu Berlin. Preussische akademie der wissenschaften: Abhandlungen: Philosophisch-historische klasse (1937, no.9): Berlin 1938. pp.102. [200.]

[W. SCHUBART], Die papyri als zeugen antiker kultur. Zugleich ein führer durch die papyrusausstellung im Neuen museum zu Berlin. [Second edition]. Berlin 1938. pp.76. [160.]

SIR HAROLD IDRIS BELL and COLIN HENDERSON ROBERTS, A descriptive catalogue of the greek papyri in the collection of Wilfred Merton. 1948–

DAVID STEWART CRAWFORD, Papyri michaelidae. Being a catalogue of the greek and latin papyri, tablets and ostraca in the library of mr. G. A. Michaïlidis of Cairo. Egypt exploration society: Aberdeen 1955. pp.xiii.166.

HERBERT KLOS, Die papyrussammlung der Österreichischen nationalbibliothek. Mit einem katalog der ständigen ausstellung. Biblos-schriften (vol.9): 1955. pp.ix.33. [52.]
— — 2. . . . . auflage. Biblos-schriften (vol.35): 1962. pp.vii.37.

A BIBLIOGRAPHY of works about papyrology. National library [Dār al-kutub al-miṣrīyah]: Cairo 1960. pp.64. [175.]

Anonymous and pseudonymous writings.

1. *Bibliographies*

ADAH V. MORRIS, Anonyms and pseudonyms. Chicago 1934. pp.[iv].22. [60.]

ARCHER TAYLOR and FREDERIC J. MOSHER, The bibliographical history of anonyma and pseudonyma. Newberry library: Chicago 1951. pp.ix. 288. [500.]

2. *General*

FRIEDRICH GEISSLER, De nominum mutatione et anonymis scriptoribus . . . dispp. Frid. Geislerus . . . et Daniel Schröck. Lipsiæ 1669. pp.[60]. [100.]

[FRIEDRICH GEISSLER], Larva detracta, h.e. brevis expositio nominum sub quibus scriptores aliquot pseudonymi recentiores imprimis latere voluerunt. Veriburgi 1670. pp.[24]. [50.]

VINCENTIUS PLACCIUS, De scriptis & scriptoribus anonymis atqve pseudonymis syntagma . . . ni quo ad sesquimille omnis generis argumenti linguarumque scripta, partim nullis, partim falsis nominibus præfixis antehac edita . . . veris auctoribus restituuntur. Hamburgi 1674. pp.[xviii]. 279. [1500.]

— — [second edition], Theatrum anonymorum et pseudonymorum, ex symbolis & collatione virorum per Europam doctissimorum . . . post syntagma dudum editum, summa beati auctoris cura reclusum, & benignis auspiciis . . . Matthiæ Dreyeri, . . . cujus & commentatio . . . accedit, luci publicæ redditum. [Edited by Ludwig Friedrich Vischer]. Hamburgi 1708. pp.[xxxv]. 722.[iv].623.195. [10,000.]

contains also Johann Deckherr, De scriptis adespotis . . . conjecturæ; *Paulus Vindingius,* Epistola de scriptis nonnullis adespotis; *Petrus Baelius* [*Pierre Bayle*], Epistola de scriptis adespotis; *Friedrich Geissler,* De nominum mutatione: *and minor essays.*

— — — Christophori Avgvsti Hevmanni de libris anonymis ac psevdonymis schediasma, complectens observationes generales et spicilegivm ad Vincentii Placcii Theatrvm anonymorvm et psevdonymorvm. Ienæ 1711. pp.[xxxii].180[*sic,* 190].[xvi]. [150.]

— — — — Bibliotheca anonymorvm et psevdonymorvm detectorvm . . . ad supplendvm et continvandvm Vincentii Placcii Theatrvm . . . et Christoph. Avgvst. Hevmanni Schediasma . . . collecta a Joh. Christoph. Mylio. Hambvrgi 1740. pp.[iv].44.viii.336.[viii].50.[xxxviii]. [4000.]

— — — — — [another issue in different format]. Hamburgi 1740. pp.[xvi].174.xxxii.1360 +[xxxii].184.[clviii]. [4000.]

JOANNES RHODIUS, Auctorum supposititiorum catalogus . . . in quo scriptores anonymi & pseudonymi complures manifestantur, opusculum posthumum ex musæo Vincentii Placcii . . . cujus etiam notæ sparsim adjectæ sunt. Hamburgi [1674]. pp.[vi].45.[xi]. [250.]

JOHANN DECKHERR, De scriptis adespotis, pseudepigraphis, et supposititiis conjecturæ. . . . [Editio secunda]. [*s.l.*] 1681. pp.[x].195.[xxvii]. [575.] *contains also the work of Vindingius.*

— — Editio tertia. Amstelædami 1686. pp. [xii].411.[xvii]. [1000.]
contains also the works of Vindingius and Bælius.

[JOHANN ALBRECHT FABRICIUS], Johannis Alberti Fabri [*sic*], Decas decadum, sive plagiariorum & pseudonymorum centuria. Lipsiæ 1689. pp.[168]. [100.]

[ADRIEN BAILLET], Auteurs deguisez, sous des noms etrangers; empruntez, supposez, feints à plaisir, chiffrez, renversez, retournez, ou changez d'une langue en une autre. 1690. pp.xxviii.615. [1750.]
other editions form part of the author's Jugemens des savans *(which is entered, as a whole, under* Bibliography: Select universal*), thus: (1722), v.I. pp.[x].241–555; (1725), v.II; (1725), V.143–350.*

PETER DAHLMANN, Schauplatz der masquirten und demasquirten gelehrten bey ihren verdeckten und nunmehro entdeckten schrifften. Leipzig 1710. pp.[xxxii].923.[lxxxiii]. [2500.]

C. W. P. G., Virorum eruditorum onomatomorphosis, das ist: Etlicher gelehrter männer gebrauchte nahmens-veränderung, insonderheit aber derjenigen, welche ihre nahmen mit griechischen wörtern verwechselt haben. Franckenhausen 1720. pp.78. [350.]

GUILLAUME FRANÇOIS DEBURE, Bibliographie instructive. Tome dixième, contenant une table destinée à faciliter la recherche des livres anonymes qui ont été annoncés par m. de Bure . . . & dans le Catalogue de m. Gaignat, & à suppléer à tout ce qui a été omis dans les tables de ces deux ouvrages. 1782. pp.xxxii.166.[ii]. [2500.]
this volume is by Jean François Née de la Rochelle.

EMIL [OTTOKAR] WELLER, Die maskirte literatur der älteren und neueren sprachen. 1. Index pseudonymorum. Leipzig 1856. pp.xi.282. [15,000.]
the main work was reissued in 1862 as a 'Zweite . . . ausgabe'.
— — Nachtraege. 1857. pp.[iv].36. [1750.]
— — Neue nachtraege. 1862. pp.[iv].72. [3750.]
— · — Drittes supplementheft. Glauchau &c. 1867. pp.iv.179. [5000.]
— — Zweite . . . auflage. Lexicon pseudonymorum. Regensburg 1886. pp.xi.627. [37,500.]

CATALOGUE alphabétique des auteurs et des ouvrages anonymes de la Bibliothèque de Neuchâtel. Neuchâtel 1861. pp.viii.112. [6000.]

OLPHAR HAMST [*pseud.* RALPH THOMAS], Handbook of fictitious names: being a guide to authors, chiefly in the lighter literature of the XIXth century, who have written under assumed names. 1868. pp.xv.236. [1750.]

a copy in the Bodleian library contains a few ms. notes.

JOHN EDWARD HAYNES, Pseudonyms of authors; including anonyms and initialisms. New York 1882. pp.112. [4000.]

FREDERICK MARCHMONT, A concise handbook of ancient and modern literature, issued either anonymously, under pseudonyms, or initials. 1896. pp.164. [2250.]

CHARLES A. STONEHILL, ANDREW BLOCK and H. WINTHROP STONEHILL, Anonyma and pseudonyma. 1926-1927. pp.vii.coll.544+1001-1502+ pp.[iii].coll.2001-2490+3001-3448. [27,500.]

325 copies printed.

3. *Countries*

America

JOSÉ TORIBIO MEDINA, Diccionario de anónimos y seudónimos hispanoamericanos. Universidad nacional: Instituto de investigaciones históricas: publicaciones (vols.xxvi-xxvii): Buenos Aires 1925. pp.xi.251+343. [3250.]

Medina left a manuscript supplement.

— — Errores y omisiones. [By] Ricardo

Victorio. Buenos Aires 1928. pp.339. [1500.]

—— Nueva epanortosis al Diccionario [&c.]. [By] Ricardo Victorio. 1929. pp.207.

further additions by Victorio appear in the Gaceta del foro *(Buenos Aires 11 abril 1930), pp.273–278.*

Argentina

LEOPOLDO DURÁN, Contribución a un diccionario de seudónimos en la Argentina. Buenos Aires 1961. pp.3–63. [600.]

VICENTE OSVALDO CUTOLO, Diccionario de alfónimos y seudónimos de la Argentina (1800–1930). Buenos Aires 1962. pp.160. [1100.]

Austria

HANS MARGREITER, Beiträge zu einem tirolischen anonymen- und pseudonymen-lexikon. 1912. pp.196. [1757.]

—— Zweite . . . auflage. Tiroler anonymen- und pseudonymen-lexikon. Archiv für bibliographie, buch- und bibliothekswesen: Beiheft (no.4): 1930 &c.

Belgium, see Netherlands

Brazil

TANCREDO DE BARROS PAIVA, Archêgas a um

diccionario de pseudonymos, iniciaes, abrevia-turas e obras anonymas de auctores brasileiros e de estrangeiros, sobre o Brasil ou no mesmo impressas. Rio de Janeiro 1929. pp.248. [1532.]
500 copies printed.

Bulgaria

IVAN BOGDANOV, Речник на българските псевдоними. София 1961. pp.354. [4000.]

Canada

HENRY SCADDING, Some canadian noms-de-plume identified. Toronto 1877. pp.57. [31.]

FRANCIS J. AUDET and GERARD MALCHELOSSE, Pseudonymes canadiens. Les dix: Montreal 1936. pp.3–191. [2000.]
300 copies printed.

Catalonia

JOSEP RODERGAS I CALMELL, Els pseudònims usats a Catalunya. Barcelona 1951. pp.xv.408. [3800.]

Colombia

RUÉEN PÉREZ ORTIZ, Seudónimos colombianos. Instituto Caro y Cuervo: Publicaciones: Serie bibliográfica (no.ii): Bogotá 1961. pp.iii–xvi.279. [2500.]

Cuba

DOMINGO FIGAROLA-CANEDA, Diccionario cubano de seudónimos. Habana 1922. pp.xvi.182. [2250.]

MANUEL GARCÍA GARÓFALO Y MESA, Diccionario de seudónimos de escritores, poetas y periodistas villaclareños. La Habana 1926. pp.61. [125.]

Denmark

C[ARL] E[MIL] SECHER, Danske anonymer og pseudonymer. Kjøbenhavn 1864. pp.66. [1000.]

E[DGAR] COLLIN, Anonymer og pseudonymer i den danske, norske og islandske literatur. Kiøbenhavn 1869. pp.[v].210. [5789.]

H[OLGER] EHRENCRON-MÜLLER, Anonym- og pseudonym-lexikon for Danmark og Island til. 1920 og Norge til 1814. København [1938–]1940 pp.[vii].392. [10,000.]

Dominica

EMILIO RODRÍGUEZ DEMORIZI, Seudónimos dominicanos. Ciudad Trujillo 1956. pp.3–283. [3000.]

Ecuador

CARLOS A. ROLANDO, Cronología del periodismo ecuatoriano. Pseudónimos de la prensa nacional. Guayaquil 1920. pp.167. [pseudonyms: 1250.]
—— [another edition]. 1934. pp.87. [1000.]

Finland

V. J. KALLIO, Fennica-kirjallisuuden salanimiä ja nimimerkkejä vuoteen 1885. Suomalaisen kirjallisuuden seuran: Toimituksia (vol.211): Helsinki 1939. pp.566. [4500.]

E. J. ELLILÄ, Kirjallisia salanimiä ja nimimerkkejä. Helsinki 1952. pp.74. [900.]

France

ANTOINE ALEXANDRE BARBIER, Dictionnaire des ouvrages anonymes et pseudonymes composés, traduits ou publiés en français. Paris 1806–1809. pp.[iii].lxxvi.522 + [iii].678 + [iii].viii.560 + [iii]. 437. [ii].lv. [12,403.]

pages 64ter–novies are inserted between pages 64 and 65 of the fourth volume; copies of this work with ms. notes by the author and by Bleuet are in the Bibliothèque nationale.

—— Seconde édition. 1822–1827. pp.[iii]. xlviii.504 + [iii].548 + [iii].684 + [iii].xxx.523. [23,647.]

copies with ms. notes by the author and others are in the Bibliothèque nationale; the fourth volume of this edition was edited by Louis Nicolas Barbier; see also the entry under Quérard, 1845, below.

—— Troisième édition, revue . . . par Olivier Barbier, René et Paul Billard. 1872–1879. pp.iii-xlvii.coll.1130 + pp.[iii].coll.1360 + pp.[iii].coll.1166+pp.[iii].1410. [50,000.]

also intended to serve as a continuation, vols.iv–vii, of the second edition of Quérard, Supercheries littéraires dévoilées, below.

——— Supplément . . . par [Pierre] Gustave Brunet. 1889. pp.[iii].iii.coll.310.pp.cxi.coll.122. pp.xiv. [4000.]

—— Additions et corrections . . . par H. [Enrico] Celani. 1902. pp.29.

[EDMOND DENIS] DE MANNE, Nouveau recueil d'ouvrages anonymes et pseudonymes. 1834. pp.vi.580.[ii]. [2131.]

—— [second edition]. Nouveau dictionnaire des ouvrages [&c.]. Lyon 1862. pp.vii.407. [3510.]

——— Retouches au Nouveau dictionnaire. Par l'auteur des Supercheries littéraires dévoilées [Joseph Marie Quérard]. 1862. pp.viii.46. [800.]

—— Troisième édition. Lyon 1868. pp.vii.607. [4616.]

J[OSEPH] M[ARIE] QUÉRARD, Les auteurs déguisés de la littérature française au XIXᵉ siècle. Essai bibliographique pour servir de supplément aux recherches d'A.-A. Barbier. 1845. pp.[iii].84. [500.]

— — [another edition]. Les supercheries littéraires dévoilées. Galerie des auteurs apocryphes, supposés, déguisés, plagiaires et des auteurs infidèles de la littérature française pendant les quatre derniers siècles. [1845-]1847-1853[-1860]. pp.cxlviii.604+650+614+668+410. [9430.]

i. *1-2, 15-16, 47-48, 91-92, 159-160, 291-292,* ii. *211-222, 263-264,* v. *137-138, 151-152 were cancelled; a copy in the Bibliothèque nationale contains both cancels and cancellands; pp.1-152 of the index were re-issued as Quérard's* Les écrivains pseudonymes, *below.*

— — Deuxième édition. Tome premier. 1865. pp.xcvi.176. [1329.]

A–Amateur only; no more published.

— — Seconde édition . . . publiée par [Pierre] Gustave Brunet et Pierre Jannet. Suivie: 1º du Dictionnaire des ouvrages anonymes par Ant. Alex. Barbier, troisième édition . . . augmentée par Olivier Barbier. . . . 2º d'une table générale des . . . deux ouvrages. 1869-1870. pp.xii.coll.1278 + pp.[iii].coll.1324 + pp.[iii].coll.1292. [20,000.]

*the third edition of Barbier is entered above, together
with the 1889 supplement by Brunet, which is intended
to serve both works; the index was not published.*

J[OSEPH] M[ARIE] QUÉRARD, Dictionnaire des
ouvrages polyonymes et anonymes de la littérature française, 1700–1845. 1846. pp.240. [2673.]

*A–Almanach musical only; no more published;
originally intended to form vols.xi–xii of* La France
littéraire, *for which purpose there is another title,
reading* La France littéraire. . . . Ouvrages polyonymes [&c.].

— — [another edition]. Les écrivains pseudonymes et autres mystificateurs de la littérature
française pendant les quatre derniers siècles. 1854.
pp.viii.152. [100.]

*A–Gerberon only; no more published; this was
another abortive attempt; it originally formed part of
vol.v of Quérard's* Les supercheries, *above.*

— — [another edition]. Les écrivains pseudonymes [&c.]. 1854–1864. pp.viii.708+[iii].752.
[25,000.]

also issued as vols.xi–xii of Quérard's France littéraire; *i. 1–152 are the same as those of the previous
entry.*

CHARLES JOLIET, Les pseudonymes du jour.

1867. pp.[v].133. [300.]
120 copies printed.
— — Nouvelle édition. 1884. pp.[v].xi.149.
[1250.]

GEORGES D'HEILLY [*pseud.* EDMOND POINSOT],
Dictionnaire des pseudonymes. 1868. pp.[viii].
141. [500.]
— — Nouvelle [third] édition. 1887. pp.[v].
iii.563. [4000.]
*in this edition the author's pseudonym appears as
d'Heylli.*

PIERRE CLAUER [*pseud.* CARLOS SOMMERVOGEL],
Une poignée de pseudonymes français recueillis
dans la Bibliotheca personata du p. Louis Jacob de
Saint-Charles. Lyon 1877. pp.27. [100.]
100 copies printed.

ROBERT [MARIE] REBOUL, Anonymes, pseudonymes et supercheries littéraires de la Provence
ancienne et moderne. Marseille 1878. pp.447.
[2355.]
100 copies printed.

J. A. VAN BEEK, Schuilnamen, naamvormen en
naamletters aangenomen door schrijvers, meest
voorkomende in de geschiedenis der Gallikaansche

en Hollandsche kerk. Rotterdam 1889. pp.16.
[275.]

EDMOND MAIGNIEN, Dictionnaire des ouvrages
anonymes et pseudonymes du Dauphiné. Bibliothèque historique du Dauphiné: Grenoble 1892.
pp.[iv].379. [2688.]

HENRY COSTON, Dictionnaire des pseudonymes.
Lectures françaises (no. spécial): [1961]. pp.260.
[6000.]

Germany

[JOHANN SAMUEL ERSCH], Verzeichniss aller
anonymen schriften und aufsätze in der vierten
ausgabe des Gelehrten Teutschlands, und deren
erstem und zweytem nachtrage. Lemgo 1788.
pp.174. [5000.]
—— Fortgesetzt aus dem dritten und vierten
nachtrage. 1794. pp.xlviii.272. [2500.]
—— Fortgesetzt aus dem fünften nachtrage.
1796. pp.[iv].114. [3000.]

FR[IEDRICH] RASSMANN, Kurzgefasstes lexicon
deutscher pseudonymer schriftsteller von der
ältern bis auf die jüngste zeit aus allen fächern der
wissenschaften. Leipzig 1830. pp.viii.248. [2500.]

ANDREAS GOTTFRIED SCHMIDT, Gallerie deutscher

pseudonymer schriftsteller vorzüglich des letzten jahrhunderts. Grimma 1840. pp.viii.254. [1500.]

ADOLPH BÜCHTING, Bibliographische nach-weisungen aus dem deutschen buchhandel. Erster jahrgang: 1866. Nordhausen 1867. pp.63. [3000.]
a bibliography of books the authorship of which is not readily apparent; no more published.

SOPHIE PATAKY, Verzeichnis der pseudonyme welche von deutschen frauen der feder seit etwa 200 jahren gebraucht worden sind. Berlin 1898. pp.[ii].72. [3500.]
also issued as part of the author's Lexicon deutscher frauen, *1898.*

MICHAEL HOLZMANN and HANNS BOHATTA, Deutsches anonymen-lexikon. Gesellschaft der bibliophilen: Weimar.

    i–iv. 1501–1850.1902–1907.pp.xvi.422+[iii]. 381+[iii].400+[v].446. [51,743.]

    v. 1851–1908. 1909. pp.vi.352. [10,811.]

    vi. 1501–1910. Nachträge und berechtigun-gen. 1911. pp.vi.335. [8508.]

    vii. 1501–1926. Nachträge und berechtigun-gen. 1928. pp.viii.504. [11,978.]

MICHAEL HOLZMANN and HANNS BOHATTA. Deutsches pseudonymen-lexikon. Wien &c. 1906, pp.[iii].xxiv.323. [19,000.]

NAMENSCHLÜSSEL. Die verweisungen zu pseudonymen, doppelnamen und namensabwandlungen. 1930. [30,000.]

— 3. ausgabe. Staatsbibliothek: Deutscher gesamtkatalog: Neue titel (1941: sonderband). Berlin 1941. pp.[vii].1019. [50,000.]

Great Britain

SAMUEL HALKETT and JOHN LAING, A dictionary of the anonymous and pseudonymous literature of Great Britain, including the works of foreigners written in or translated into the english language. [Edited by Catherine Laing]. Edinburgh 1882–1888. pp.[iii].3.coll.870. pp.[ii]+[iii].coll.871–1762.pp.[i]+[iii].coll.1763–2596.+pp.6.coll.2595–2852.ccccxxiv. [15,000.]

— — New . . . edition. By James Kennedy, W. A. Smith and A. F[orbes] Johnson. Edinburgh &c. 1926–1934. pp.xxviii.472 + [iii].421 + [iii].412 + [iii].463 + [iii].406 + [v].449 + [v].588. [60,000.]

— — — Supplement, 1900–1950. By Dennis Everard Rhodes and Anna Elisabeth Charlotte Simoni.

WILLIAM CUSHING, Initials and pseudonyms: a dictionary of literary disguises. New York 1885.

pp.iv.603. [10,000.]
also issued in 1886 with a London imprint; includes a few foreign entries.

WILLIAM CUSHING, Anonyms. Cambridge, U.S.A. 1889. pp.[iii].400+[ii].401–829. [27,500.]
also issued in 1890 with a London imprint.

[ALFRED] COTGREAVE, A selection of pseudo-nyms, or fictitious names, used by well known authors, with real names given. Also a number of anonymous works with the authors given. 1891. pp.24. [900.]

WILLIAM PRIDEAUX COURTNEY, The secrets of our national literature. Chapters in the history of the anonymous and pseudonymous writings of our countrymen. 1908. pp.vii.255. [750.]

WILLIAM ABBATT, The colloquial who's who. An attempt to identify the many authors ... who have used pen-names, initials, etc. (1600–1924). Vol.II. Great Britain and Colonies. Tarrytown, N.Y. 1925. pp.[ii].137. [5500.]
— — Appendix II. 1928. pp.10. [400.]
— — [Appendix 3]. 1931. pp.12. [400.]
— — Appendix no.4. 1934. pp.2. [63.]
no appendix 1 was issued for this volume; appendixes 3 and 4 are respectively on blue and pink paper.

Anonymous Writings

Hebrew

JOH[ANN] DAVID HOHEISEL, Pseudonymorum hebraicorum hexecontas. Gedani [1708]. pp.34. [60.]

[GABRIEL GRODDECK], לקט פלוגי אלמוגי id est spicilegium aliquot librorum anonymorum et pseudonymorum, qui lingua rabbinica partim impressi, partim manuscripti reperiuntur. Trajecti ad Rhenum 1728. pp.196. [519.]

W[ILHELM] ZEITLIN, Anagramme, initialen und pseudonyma neu-hebräischer schriftsteller und publizisten. Frankfurt a.M. 1905. pp.18. [400.]

SAUL CHAJES, רעואי הוישמ בלוייאוע השם. Thesaurus pseudonymorum quæ in litteratura hebraica et judaeo-germanica inveniuntur. Israelitisch-theologische lehranstalt: Veröffentlichungen der Oberrabbiner dr. H. P. Chajes-preisstiftung [vol.iv]: Wien 1933. pp.xiv.335. ד [vi].66. [2500.]

Hungary

DÁVID SZÉKELY, Magyar írók álnevei a multban és jelenben. Budapest 1904. pp.71. [2750.]

PÁL GULYÁS, Magyar írói álnév lexikon. A magyarországi írók álnevei és egyéb jegyei. Budapest 1956. pp.706. [20,000.]

Iceland, see *Denmark*

Italy

GIO: PIETRO GIACOMO VILLANI [*pseud.* LODOVICO (*in religion:* ANGELICO) APROSIO], La visiera alzata. Hecatoste di scrittori che vaghi d'andare in maschera fuor del tempo di carnovale. Parma 1689. pp.136. [500.]

VINCENZO LANCETTI, Pseudonimia, ovvero tavole alfabetiche de' nomi finti o supposti degli scrittori, con la contrapposizione de' veri. Milano 1836. pp.[vii].l.449. [7500.]

G. M. [COUNT GAETANO MELZI], Dizionario di opere anonime e pseudonime di scrittori italiani o come che sia aventi relazione all' Italia. Milano 1848-1859. pp.[iii].482 + [iii].483 + xvi.701. [8000.]

—— Supplemento ... da Giambattista Passano. Ancona 1887. pp.xi.517. [2000.]

—— Anonimi e pseudonimi italiani. Supplemento al Melzi e al Passano ... da E[mmanuele] Rocco. Napoli 1888. pp.16. [100.]

a photographic reprint of the whole was issued New York 1960–1961, and Cosenza 1961.

[COUNT] GIAMBATTISTA CARLO GIULIARI, La pseudonimia veronese. Verona 1881. pp.58. [400.]

[GIOVANNI] BATTISTA MONTAROLO, Bibliografia del Risorgimento italiano. Opere anonime e pseudonime. Rome 1884. pp.38. [250.]
200 copies printed.

COUNT G. B. C. [GIAMBATTISTA CARLO GIULIARI], Gli anonimi veronesi. Verona 1885. pp.192. [1292.]

RENZO FRATTAROLO, Anonimi e pseudonimi. Repertorio delle bibliografie nazionali, con un dizionario degli scrittori italiani (1900–1954). Roma [1955]. pp.211. [anonyms &c.: 1000.]

ALDO SANTI, Dizionario pseudonimico degli enigmografi italiani. Modena 1956. pp.141. [3000.]

Latin

ALFRED [LOUIS AUGUSTE] FRANKLIN, Dictionnaire des noms, surnoms, et pseudonymes latins de l'histoire littéraire du moyen âge (1100 à 1530). 1875. pp.xi.coll.640.pp.641–684. [9000.]

Luxemburg

CARLO HURY, Dictionnaire de pseudonymes d'auteurs luxembourgeois. Bibliographia luxemburgensis (no.2): Luxembourg 1960. pp.17. [350.]

Anonymous Writings

Mexico

JUAN B[AUTISTA] IGUÍNIZ, Catálogo de seudónimos, anagramas e iniciales de escritores mexicanos. París &c. 1913. pp.62. [500.]

JUANA MANRIQUE DE LARA and GUADELUPE MONROY, Seudónimos, anagramas, iniciales, etc., de autores mexicanos y extranjeros. Secretaría de educación pública: México 1943. pp.78. [1000.]

—— Seconda edición. 1954. pp.117. [1500.]

ROBERTO VALLES, Índice de anonimos de la Bibliografía mexicana del siglo XVIII del dr. don Nicolás León. Biblioteca aportación historica: México 1946. pp.44. [750.]

150 copies printed.

Netherlands and Belgium

[JULES VICTOR DE LE COURT], Essai d'un dictionnaire des ouvrages anonymes et pseudonymes publiés en Belgique au XIXᵉ siècle et principalement depuis 1830. Par un membre de la Société des bibliophiles belges. Bruxelles 1863. pp.550. [3200.]

100 copies printed.

—— Bibliographie nationale. Dictionnaire des anonymes et pseudonymes (XVᵉ siècle–1900). Aca-

démie royale de Belgique: Bruxelles 1960–
pp.xii.1281.10+
in progress.

J[AN] I[ZAAK] VAN DOORNINCK, Bibliotheek
van nederlandsche anonymen en pseudonymen.
's Gravenhage &c. [1867–1870]. pp.xii.coll.838.
pp.[ii]. [6452.]

—— Tweede uitgave Vermomde en naam-
looze schrijvers opgespoord op het gebied der
nederlandsche en vlaamsche letteren. Leiden
[1881–]1883–1885.   pp.[iv].coll.672+pp.[ii].coll.
678.pp.[iii]. [8000.]

—— Vervolg . . . door A[afke de Kempe-
naer. [1928]. pp.[vii].coll.694. [10,000.]

V[ICTOR] A[LEXIS] DELA MONTAGNE, Vlaamsche
pseudoniemen. Bibliographische opzoekingen.
Roeselaere 1884. pp.xiii.132. [500.]
150 copies printed.

J. A. VAN BEEK, Schuilnamen, naamvormen en
naamletters aangenomen door schrijvers, meest
voorkomende in de geschiedenis der Gallikaansche en Hollandsche kerk. Rotterdam 1889.
pp.16. [275.]

C. T. TUYMELAAR, Pseudoniemen uit de neder-

landsche en buitenlandsche literatuur. Assen
1937. pp.40. [400.]
limited in the main to contemporary writers.

Norway, see also *Denmark*

HJALMAR PETTERSEN, Anonymer og pseudonymer i den norske literatur, 1678–1890. Kristiania
1890. pp.[iv].coll.128. [2000.]
— — [second edition]. Norsk anonym- og
pseudonym-lexicon. 1924. pp.[viii].coll.690.
pp.[xxxiv]. [6000.]

GUSTAV E[LISAR] RAABE, Anonymer og pseudonymer i Årskatalog over norsk litteratur. [Oslo].
1926–1930. [1932]. pp.32 [225.]
1931–1935. 1940. pp.48. [150.]

W[ILHELM] P[REUS] SOMMERFELDT, Forfatter-
merker i norske aviser og tidsskrifter, 1931–1935.
Norsk bibliografisk bibliotek (vol.ii, no.2): Oslo
1936. pp.20. [1750.]
— — Tweede utgave.... (vol.viii): 1946. pp.31.
[1750.]

Poland

EDWARD MINKOWIECKI, Wykaz pseudonymów
używanych autorów polskich. . . . Wydanie
drugie. Warszawa 1888. pp.xxxii. [1500.]

Anonymous Writings

J. Z[BIEGNIEWSKA], Pseudonimy i kriptonimy pisarzów polskich. Książki dla wszystkich [no.153]: Warszawa 1905. pp.160. [2000.]

H. D[ABCZAŃSKA-BUDZYNOWSKA], Pseudonimy pisarzy polskich. Lwów 1910. pp.160. [2250.]

L[UDWIK] CZARKOWSKI, Pseudonimy i kryptonimy polskie. Wilne 1922. pp.170. [1750.]

ADAM BAR, Słownik pseudonimów i kryptonimów pisary polskich oraz Polski dotyczących. Krakowskie koło: Związek bibljotekarzy polskich: Prace bibljoteczne (vols.vii–ix): Kraków 1936–1938. pp.xxxix.231+[iv].240+[iv].150. [12,500.]

Portugal

MARTINHO AUGUSTO [FERREIRA] DA FONSECA, Subsidios para um diccionario de pseudonymos, inicaes e obras anonymas de escriptores portuguezes. Lisboa 1896. pp.xiii.299. [2400.]

Russia

P. BIBLIOGRAF [*pseud.*], Показатепь псевдонимовъ. Казань 1868. pp.[iv].6. [26.]

G. G. [GRIGORY NIKOLAEVICH GENNADI], Списокърусскихъ анонимныхъ книгъ съ именами ихъ авторовъ и переводчиковъ. С.-Петербургъ 1874. pp.[ii].iii.47. [750.]

V[ASILY] S[ERGYEEVICH] KARTSOV and M[IKHAIL] N[IKOLAEVICH] MAZAEV, Опытъ словаря псевдонимовъ русскихъ писателей. С.-Петербургъ 1891. pp.[vi].158. [5000.]

additions appear in Библиографическія записки *(1892), pp.123–126, 370–372, 429–443, 813–816.*

I[VAN] F[ILIPPOVICH] MASANOV, Словарь псевдонимов русских писателей, ученых и общественных деятелей. Москва 1941–1949. pp.xlvii.coll.571+pp.vii.coll.836. [25,000.]

—— [another edition]. Подготовил к печати Ю. И. Масанов. Редактор Б. П. Козьмин. 1956–1960. pp.444+388+416+559. [70,000.]

DIMITRY M[IKHAILOVICH] KRASSOVSKY, Russian pseudonyms, initials, etc. Materials for the dictionary. Hoover library [&c.]: Stanford [1948]. ff.[iii].vii.307. [5000.]*

Slovakia

JÁN V[LADIMÍR] ORMIS, Slovník slovenskych pseudonymov. Slovenske národne knižnice: Turč. sv. Martine 1944. pp.3–369. [2000.]

JAROSLAV KUNC, Vlastním jménem. Slovníček pseudonymů novodobých českých spisovatelů.

Národní knihovna: Bibliografický katalog ČSR: Praze 1958. pp.68. [2000.]

[ŠTEFAN HANAKOVIČ], Slovník pseudonymov slovenských spisovateľov. Matica slovenská: Martine 1961. pp.336. [5000.]*

Spain

MAXIRIRIARTH [*pseud.* EUGENIO HARTZENBUSCH], Unos cuantos seudónimos españoles con sus correspondientes nombres verdaderos. Madrid 1892. pp.56. [900 names.]

—— Edición . . . aumentada. 1904. pp.xix.169. [1500 titles.]

EDUARDO PONCE DE LEÓN FREYRE and FLORENTINO ZAMORA LUCAS, 1.500 seudónimos modernos de la literatura española (1900–1942). Instituto nacional del libro español: Madrid 1942. pp.126. [1500.]

Sweden

ANDREAS ANTONIUS [ANDERS ANTON] STIERNMAN, Anonymorum centuria prima [-secunda] ex scriptoribus gentis Sviogothicæ. Holmæ 1724–1726. pp.[viii].53.[iii]+[viii].152. [200.]

[C. EICHHORN], Upptäckta svenska pseudonymer och homonymer. Stockholm 1859. pp.12. [2000.]

[ANDERS] LEONARD BYGDÉN, Svenskt anonym-
och pseudonym-lexicon. Skrifter utgifna af
Svenska litteratursällskapet (vol.xvii): Upsala
1898–1915.   pp.[ii].v.ix.coll.944+pp.[iii].coll.
1052.pp.ii. [15,000.]

United States

WILLIAM ABBATT, The colloquial who's who.
An attempt to identify the many authors . . . who
have used pen-names, initials, &c. (1600–1924).
Vol.I. The United States and Canada. Tarrytown,
N.Y. 1924. pp.109. [3000.]
—— Appendix II. [1924]. pp.[2]. [17.]
—— Appendix III. 1928. pp.9. [350.]
—— Appendix 5. 1934. pp.9. [350.]
*appendix 1 forms part of the main work; no appen-
dix 4 was issued for this volume; appendixes 3 and 5
are respectively on blue and pink paper.*

LILLIE BROOKS, Dictionary of pseudonyms and
sobriquets. Bakersfield, Cal. [1963]. pp.[ii].47.
[1750.]

Uruguay

ARTURO SCARONE, Apuntes para un diccionario
de seudónimos y de publicaciones anónimas.
Biblioteca nacional: Montevideo 1926. pp.75.
[147.]

—— Segunda edición. 1934. pp.xvi.353. [732.]

—— Segunda [*sic*] edición. Diccionario de seudónimos del Uruguay. 1942. pp.632. [1684.]

4. *Miscellaneous*

[JOHANN CHRISTOPH SIEBENKEES], Apocalypsis CL iureconsultorum et scriptorum iuris pseudo-nymorum collecta a Philalethe. Solisbaci 1806. pp.47. [150.]

[HENRY FOLEY], Alphabetical catalogue of members of the english province S.J. [Society of Jesus], who assumed aliases or by-names, together with the said aliases. By a member of the same society. English province S.J.: [*s.l.*] 1875. pp.[ii]. 32.[ii]. [1250.]

privately printed; the last leaf, numbered 293–294, is a supplement; a copy in the Bodleian library contains ms. additions.

DIEGO BARROS ARANA, Notas para una biblio-grafía de obras anónimas i seudónimas sobre la historia, la jeografía i la literatura de América. Santiago de Chile 1882. pp.171. [507.]

CARLOS SOMMERVOGEL, Dictionnaire des ouvrages anonymes et pseudonymes publiés par des religieux de la Compagnie de Jésus. 1884. pp.[iii].iii.coll.1398.pp.[iii]. [7500.]

Anonymous Writings

ALPHABETISCHES verzeichniss der in Kloss'
Bibliographie der freimaurerei und Taute's Mau-
rerischer bücherkunde angeführten anonymen
schriften. München 1898. pp.[iii].95. [5000.]

J[OSÉ] EUG[ENIO] URIARTE, Catálogo razonado
de obras anónimas y seudónimas de autores de la
Compañía de Jésus pertenecientes á la antigua
asistencia española. Madrid 1904–1916. pp.xxxii.
527+615+xii.651+vii.606+xxvii.653. [7000.]

Condemned books.

[*editions of the official roman catholic indexes are excluded.*]

Condemned Books

1. General

[ÉTIENNE] G[ABRIEL] PEIGNOT, Dictionnaire critique, littéraire et bibliographique des principaux livres condamnés au feu, supprimés ou censurés. 1806.pp.xvi.xl.343+[ii].295. [1000.]

supplements appear in Le bibliophile belge, 1848–1850.

ANNE LYON HAIGHT, Banned books: informal notes on some books banned for various reasons at various times and in various places. New York 1935. pp.[viii].104. [300.]

—— [another edition]. London 1935. pp.xix. 172. [300.]

—— Second edition. 1955. pp.xix.172. [500.]

MAX IVERSEN and ÅSE HENRIKSEN, Forbudte bøger. To aarhundreders beslaglagte og konfiskerede værker. En annoteret bibliografi. København 1948. pp.199. [250.]

limited to Scandinavia, England, France and Germany; 500 copies printed.

2. Countries

America

DOROTHY SCHONS, Book censorship in New

Spain. New world studies (vol.ii): Austin, Texas
1949. pp.xviii.45. [112.]*
a calendar of documents; 200 copies printed.

Austria [see also *Germany*]

CATALOGUS librorum, a Commissione aulica
prohibitorum. Vindobonae 1765. pp.184. [2750.]
— Supplementum. 1771. pp.55. [750.]
— Editio nova. Vienæ Austriæ 1774. pp.364.
[4000.]

ANTON EINSLE, Catalogus librorum in Austria
prohibitorum. Verein der österr.-ungar. buchhändler: Publicationen (vol.viii): Wien 1896. pp.
xxxii.159. [3500.]
— — Supplementum 1. . . . Von Carl Junker. . . .
(vol.x): 1902. pp.viii.45. [700.]
500 copies privately printed.

LISTE der gesperrten autoren und bücher. Bun-
desministerium für unterricht: [Wien] 1946. pp.
74. [2250.]

Czechoslovakia

[ANTONÍN KONIÁŠ], Index bohemicorum librorum prohibitorum, et corrigendorum ordine
alphabeti digestus. Vetero-Pragæ [*c.*1775]. pp.
[lxxix].320. [2500.]

Condemned Books

FRANTIŠEK LOSKOT, O indexech zakázaných knih. (Index římský a indexy české). Knihovna Volné Myšlenky (2nd series, vol.iii): Praha 1911. pp.59. [500.]

France

CATALOGUS librorvm qvi hactenus à Facultate theologiæ parisiensi diligenter examinati, censuraꝗ digni visi sunt. Antverpiae 1545. pp.[62]. [250.]

LE CATALOGUE des livres examinez, & cēsurez par la Faculté de théologie de l'vniuersité de Paris, depuis l'an mil cinq cents quarante & quatre, iusques à l'an present, suyuāt l'edict du roy, donné à Chasteau Briant. 1551. pp.[104]. [500.]

— — Auquel sont adioustez ceulx qui ont été censurez depuis la première impression. 1556. pp. [120]. [600.]

INDEX expvrgatorius librorvm qvi hoc secvlo prodiervnt, vel doctrinæ non sanæ erroribus inspersis, vel inutilis & offensiuæ maledicentiæ fellibus permixtis, iuxta sacri Concilij Tridentini decretum . . . concinnatus; anno MDLXXI. Nunc primùm in lucem editus, & præfatione auctus ac regij diplomatis interpretatione. Lugdunensem 1586. pp.[lx].292. [100.]

ARRESTS du Parlament et ordonnances de monseigneur l'archevesque de Paris, portant la deffense & suppression des livres heretiques. 1685. pp.91. [iv]. [750.]

[— MAYNARD DE FRANC], Catalogue des ouvrages condamnés depuis 1814 jusqu'à ce jour. 1827. pp.76.70. [100.]

CATALOGUE alphabétique des ouvrages condamnés, ou relevé de toutes les publications officielles faites au Moniteur, en exécution de la loi du 26 mai 1819. 1836. pp.74.38. [200.]

[JEAN BAPTISTE BOONE], Les mauvais livres, les mauvais journaux et les romans. Troisième édition. Bruxelles [1842]. pp.142. [250.]
— — Quatrième édition. [c.1845]. pp.267. [1000.]
the earlier editions were not bibliographical.

CATALOGUE des ouvrages qui ont été l'objet soit de condamnations, soit de poursuites judiciaires, depuis 1814. 1843. pp.[iii].86. [500.]
— [another edition]. Catalogue des écrits, gravures et dessins condamnés depuis 1814 jusqu'au 1er janvier 1850. 1850. pp.[iii].iv.203. [600.]
— [another edition]. Catalogue des ouvrages

condamnés . . . 1814 . . . [to] 1873. 1874. pp.112. [600.]

— [another edition]. Catalogue des ouvrages, écrits et dessins de toute nature poursuivis, supprimés ou condamnés depuis le 21 octobre 1814 jusqu'au 31 juillet 1877. Édition . . . nouvelle . . . par Fernand Drujon [1878–]1879. pp.[ii].xxxvii. 430. [1250.]

E. DE FRÉVILLE, De la police des livres au xviᵉ siècle. Livres et chansons mis à l'index par l'inquisiteur de la province ecclésiastique de Toulouse (1548–1549). 1853. pp.38. [92.]
100 copies printed.

ОБЩІЙ, алфавитный списокъ книгамъ на французскомъ языкѣ, запрещеннымъ иностранною цензурою безусловно и для публики съ 1815 по 1853 годъ включительно. Санктпетербургъ 1855. pp.[ii].387. [2895.]

[P. E. A. POULET-MALASSIS], Bulletin trimestriel des publications défendues en France, imprimées à l'étranger. [Bruxelles] 1867–1869. pp.[36]. [141.]
published in 8 nos.; the British museum copy has a ms. index.

[TIBULLE] DESBARREAUX-BERNARD, L'inquisition des livres à Toulouse au xviiᵉ siècle. Toulouse [1874]. pp.54. [99.]

JEAN GAY, Šaisie de livres prohibés faite aux Couvents des Jacobins et des Cordeliers à Lyon, en 1694. Nouvelle édition augmentée d'un répertoire bibliographique. Turin 1876. pp.88. [250.] *300 copies printed.*

JULES ANDRIEU, La censure et la police des livres en France sous l'ancien régime. Une saisie de livres à Agen en 1775. Agen 1884. pp.47. [46.]

R[OGER] V[ALLENTIN DU] C[HEYLARD], Suppression de quelques ouvrages (1759–1785). Grenoble [printed] 1911. pp.16. [15.]

LISTE Otto. Ouvrages retirés de la vente par les éditeurs ou interdits par les autorités allemandes. [1940]. pp.[13]. [1500.]
—[another edition]. Ouvrages littéraires fráncais non désirables. Syndicat des éditeurs: [1942]. pp.15. [1500.]
— Unerwünschte literatur in Frankreich. [3. . . . auflage. Mit einem anhang der namen jüdischer autoren in französischer sprache.] [Syndicat des éditeurs de Paris: 1943]. pp.27.

DANIEL BECOURT, Livres condamnés, livres interdits. [1961]. pp.155. [1500.]

MARCELIN DEFOURNEAUX, L'inquisition espa-

gnole et les livres français au XVIIIe siècle. 1963.
pp.[vi].215. [400.]

Germany

LIBRORVM avthorvmqve s. Sedis Apostolicæ,
sacriqve concilij Tridentini avthoritate prohibitorvm. Itemqve eorvm ex quibus integra bibliotheca
catholica institui rectè possit indices dvo. Pro
vsu monasteriorvm in Bauaria editi. Monachii
1569. pp.[98]. [1500.]

INDEX expvrgatorivs librorvm qvi hoc sæcvlo
prodiervnt, vel doctrinæ non sanę erroribus
inspersis, vel inutilis & offensivæ maledicentæ fellibus permixtis, iuxta sacri Concilij Tridentini
decretum: Philippi II. Regis Catholici iussu &
auctoritate, atq; Albani Ducis consilio ac ministe-
tio in Belgia concinatus; anno M D LXXI. [Stras-
burg] 1599. pp.[lxxvi].363. [100.]

— [another edition]. Argentorati 1609. pp.
[xxx].521. [150.]

NEU durchgesehenes verzeichniss der verbothe-
nen deutschen bücher. Wien 1816. pp.[ii].350.
[4500.]

L. BRANDT, Das reichsgesetz gegen die gemeingefährlichen bestrebungen der sozialdemokratie
vom 21. Oktober 1878, nebst ... einem alphabeti-

schen verzeichniss der verbotenen druckschriften. Berlin 1882. pp.[iii].144. [750.]

OTTO ATZROTT, Sozial-demokratische druckschriften und vereine verboten auf grund des reichsgesetzes gegen die gemeingefährlichen bestrebungen der sozialdemokratie vom 21. Oktober 1878. Berlin 1886. pp.viii.111.

—— Nachtrag. 1888. pp.vii.46.

VERZEICHNIS der verbotenen bücher und zeitschriften, 1903 bis ende März 1914. Börsenverein der deutschen buchhändler: Leipzig 1914. pp.78. [1000.]

H[EINRICH] H[UBERT] HOUBEN, Verbotene literatur von der klassischen zeit bis zur gegenwart. Ein kritisch-historisches lexicon über verbotene bücher, zeitschriften und theaterstücke, schriftsteller und verleger. Berlin 1924. pp.168. [500.]

—— Zweite verbesserte auflage. 1925–1928. pp.623+616. [1000.]

LISTE der von der Interalliierten Rheinlandkommission in Coblenz für das besetzte gebiet verbotenen bücher, lichtbildstreifen und zeitungen. Reichsministerium für die besetzten gebiete: Berlin 1925. pp.39. [752.]

ERNST DRAHN, Verbotene und undeutsche bücher. Ein führer zur völkischen gestaltung der deutschen leihbüchereien. Berlin 1933. pp.19. [450.]

LISTE des schädlichen und unerwünschten schrifttums. Reichsschrifttumskammer: Leipzig [printed] [1939]. pp.[iv].181. [5500.]

— — [supplement]. Jahresliste ... des schädlichen und unerwünschten schrifttums. [Reichsschrifttumskammer:] Leipzig.

    1939. pp.12. [150.]
    1940. pp.22. [350.]
    1941. pp.22. [350.]
no more published; marked 'streng vertraulich'.

LISTE der für jugendliche und büchereien ungeeigneten druckschriften. Reichsministerium für volksaufklärung und propaganda: Schriftenreihe des Grossdeutschen leihbüchereiblattes (no.2): Leipzig 1941. pp.77. [1750.]

— 2. [*sic*] ... auflage. .... Schriftenreihe des Deutschen büchereiblattes (no.2): 1943. pp.127. [1750.]

    the second edition appeared in 1942; this is the third.

BOOKS the nazis banned. An exhibition in the New York public library. [New York 1942]. pp.11. [100.]

Condemned Books

LISTE der für jugendliche und büchereien ungeeigneten druckschriften. 2. Veränderte auflage.
Reichsministerium für volksauf klärung und propaganda: Schriftenreihe des Deutschen büchereiblattes (no.2): Leipzig 1943. pp.127.
—— [another edition]. 1946. pp.183. [4000.]
——— Nachtrag.
  i. 1947. pp.179. [4000.]
  ii. 1948. pp.366. [9906.]

LISTE der auszusondernden literatur. Vorläufige
ausgabe. Deutsche verwaltung für volksbildung
in der sowjetischen besatzungszone. Berlin 1946.
pp.528. [13,000.]

Great Britain

WILLIAM HENRY HART, Index expurgatorius
anglicanus, or a descriptive catalogue of the principal books printed or published in England, which
have been suppressed, or burnt by the common
hangman, or censured, or for which the authors,
printers, or publishers have been prosecuted. 1872–
1878. pp.290. [294.]
*covers the period 1524–1683; incomplete; no more
published.*

JAMES ANSON FARRER, Books condemned to be
burnt. Book-lover's library: 1892. pp.xii.207.[100.]
reissued 1904.

Condemned Books

CHARLES RIPLEY GILLETT, Burned books. Neglected chapters in british history and literature. New York 1932. pp.xiii.356+[vii].357-725. [650.]

Hebrew

GUSTAVO SACERDOTE, Deux index expurgatoires de livres hébreux. Versailles 1895. pp.31. [65.]

Ireland

BOOKS prohibited in the Irish Free State under the Censorship of publications act, 1929. Dublin [1933]. pp.27. [325.]*
— [another edition]. Books prohibited in Eire [&c.]. 1940. pp.38. [1250.]
— [another edition]. [1948]. pp.[ii].66. [1500.]
— — Supplementary list.
   1948-1949.

Italy

[GIOVANNI DELLA CASA], Il catalogo de libri li qvali nvovamente . . . sono stati condannati, & scomunicati per heretici da M. Giouan della casa. legato di Vinetia, & d'alcuni frati. E'aggivnto sopra il medesimo catalogo vn iudicio, & discorso del [Pietro Paolo] Vergerio. [?Venice] 1549. pp. [167]. [150.]

CATALOGVS librorvm haereticorvm qvi hactenvs

colligi potuerñt a uiris catholicis, supplendus in dies, si qui alij ad notitiam deuenerint, de commissione tribunalis, sanctissimae inquisitionis Venetiarum. Venetiis 1554. pp.[38]. [400.]

— [another edition]. Venetiis 1554. pp.31. [600.]

ELENCHI di opere la cui pubblicazione, diffusione o ristampa nel regno è stata vietata dal Ministero della cultura popolare. Roma 1940. pp.85. [1750.]

Mexico

DOCUMENTOS para la historia de la cultura en México. . . . Catálogo de libros expurgados a los jesuítas en el siglo XVIII. Archivo general de la nación and Universidad nacional autónoma: Publicaciones (no.3): México 1947. pp.xiii.193. [100.]

Netherlands and Belgium

DIE CATALOGEN of inventaryen van den quaden verboden bouken: na advis der universiteyt van Louen. Louen 1510.

MANDAMĒT der keyserlijcker maiesteit, vuytghegeuē int iaer xlvi. Met dintitulatie ende declaratie vandē gereprobeerde boecken, gheschiet bijden doctoren inde Faculteyt van theologie in duniuersiteyt van Loeuen, duer dordonnantie ende beuel der seluer k̰ m. Loeuen 1546. pp.[77]. [200.]

also issued in a french edition; 100 copies of a facsimile were issued [by the Hispanic society of America], New York [in 1896].

CATALOGI librorū reprobatorvm, et praelegendorum ex indicio Academiæ louaniensis. Lovanii 1550. pp.[24]. [250.]

— Die catalogen oft inuentarisen vanden quaden verboden boucken: ende van andere goede, diemen den iongē scholieren leeren mach, na aduys der uniuersiteyt van Loeuen. Loeuen 1550. pp.[35]. [250.]

— Les catalogues des liures reprouuez, et de ceulx que lon pourra enseigner par laduis de luniuersité de Louuain. Lovvain 1550. pp.[23]. 250.]

— [another latin edition]. Toleti 1551. pp.[32]. [400.]

— [another latin edition]. Pinciæ 1551. pp.[24]. [500.]

100 copies of a facsimile of each of the 1551 editions were issued [by the Hispanic society of America], New York [in 1893].

CATALOGUE des livres défendus par la Commis-

sion impériale et royale jusqu'à l'année 1786.
Bruxelles 1788. pp.[ii].91. [1000.]

A[BRAHAM] J[ACOBUS] SERVAAS VAN ROOIJEN,
Verboden boeken, geschriften, couranten, enz.
in de 18ᵉ eeuw. Eene bijdrage tot de geschiedenis
der haagsche censuur.... 1ᵉ[-2ᵉ] aflevering. Haar-
lem 1881–1882. pp.96. [50.]
 1700–1746 only; no more published.

CHRISTIAAN SEPP, Verboden lectuur. Een drietal
indices librorum prohibitorum toegelicht. Leiden
1889. pp.[viii].286. [1000.]
 *a bibliographical index of the lists published in the
Netherlands in 1550–1570.*

W[ILLEM] P[IETER] C[ORNELIS] KNUTTEL, Verboden boeken in de republiek der Vereenigde
Nederlanden. Beredeneerde catalogus. Bijdragen
tot de geschiedenis van den nederlandschen boek-
handel (vol.xi): 's-Gravenhage 1914. pp.xii.140.
[450.]

ÉMILE FAIRON, Le premier index de livres prohibés à Liége, 1545. Anvers [1925]. pp.19. [100.]

Poland

Z. CELICHOWSKI, Polskie indeksy książek
zakazanych. Rozprawa bibliograficzna. Kraków
1899. pp.11. [3.]

Russia

P[ETR] I[VANOVICH] BERNOV, *ed.* Справочный указатель книгъ и журналовъ, арестованныхъ съ 17 октября 1905 г. по 1 января 1909 г. Москва 1909. pp.160. [2400.]

L[EV] M[IKHAILOVICH] DOBROVOLSKY, Запрещенная книга в России, 1825–1904 Архивно-библиографические разыскания. Москва 1962. pp.255. [248.]

Spain

CATHALOGVS librorũ, qui prohibẽtur mandato illustrissimi & reuerend. d. d. Ferdinandi de Valdes Hispaleñ. archiepĩ, inquisitoris generalis Hispaniæ. Pinciæ 1559. pp.27 [*sic*, 72]. [750.]
100 copies of a facsimile were issued [by the Hispanic society of America], New York [in 1895].

INDEX librorvm prohibitorvm et expvrgatorvm ... Bernardi de Sandoval et Roxas ... cardin. ... Hispaniorvm primatis ... generalis inqvisitoris ... avctoritate et ivssv editvs. Madriti 1612. pp.[x]. 102.[xxx].739.[iv]. [2500.]
the titlepage is engraved.
— Appendix prima. 1614. pp.[viii].42.[ii]. [200.]
— Appendix secvnda. 1628. pp.[vii].51. [200.]

A[NTONIO] PAZ Y MEL'IA, Papeles de inquisición. Catálogo y extractos. Segunda edición por Ramón Paz [Remolar]. Archivo histórico nacional: Madrid 1947. pp.3-530. [1511.]
the first edition was published in the Revista de archivos, *1907-1914.*

ANTONIO SIERRA CORELLA, La censura de libros y papeles en España y los índices y catálogos de los prohibidos y expurgados. Cuerpo facultativo de archiveros, bibliotecarios y arqueologos: Madrid 1947. pp.362. [265.]

TRES indices expurgatorios de la inquisición española en el sigli XVI. Real academia española (2nd ser., vol.v): Madrid 1952. pp.[124].
consists of facsimiles of the above 1559 list, and of the 1551 catalogues entered above under the Netherlands; 300 copies printed.

MARCELIN DEFOURNEAUX, L'inquisition espagnole et les livres français au XVIIIᵉ siècle. 1963. pp.[vi].215. [400.]

Sweden

SAMUEL J. ALNANDER, Historia librorum prohibitorum in Svecia. Upsaliæ 1764. pp.[iv].36. [30.]
limited to the 17th century.

Condemned Books

3. Roman catholic

i. Bibliographies

J[ULIUS] PETZHOLDT, Catalogus 'Indicis librorum prohibitorum et expurgandorum'. Dresdae 1859. pp.34. [250.]

WILLIAM I[RELAND] KNAPP, Official editions and reprints of the Index librorum prohibitorum issued in the sixteenth century. New-York 1880. pp.8. [150.]

a copy containing ms. notes and additions, with special reference to the Bodleian, is in that library.

F[RIEDRICH] H[EINRICH] REUSCH, Die Indices librorum prohibitorum et expurgandorum des 16. jahrhunderts. Dresden [1880]. pp.10. [75.]

ii. General

GIOVANNI MARIA [GUANZELLI], Indicis librorvm expvrgandorvm in studiosorum gratiam confecti tomus primus.... Per fr. Io. Mariam Brasichellen. ... in vnum corpus redactus. Romae 1607. pp. [xvi].743. [100.]

—— [another edition]. Bergomi 1608. pp.608. [100.]

THO[MAS] JAMES, Index generalis librorvm prohibitorvm à Pontificiis ... in usum Bibliothecæ bodleianæ . . . designatus. Oxoniæ 1627. pp.[235]. [2500.]

FRANCISCUS MAGDALENUS CAPIFERREUS, Elenchvs librorvm omnivm tum in Tridentino, Clementinoq. indice, tum in alijs omnibus sacræ indicis congreg.^{nis} particularibus decretis hactenus prohibitorum. Romae 1632. pp.[vii].679. [10,000.]

— — — Editio secunda. 1640. pp.[vii].412. [11,000.]

DANIEL FRANCKE, Danielis Franci Disqvisitio academica de papistarum indicibus librorum prohibitorum et expurgandorum. Lipsiæ 1684. pp. [xxxvi].226.[xlix]. [2000.]

ANDREAS WESTPHAL, Epistola I. ad fratrem Christianum Westphalium, qua libri publica auctoritate combusti recensentur atque exhibentur. Sedini 1709. pp.[24]. [50.]

— — Epistola II. ad fratrem Christianum Westphalium, sistens decadem librorum publica auctoritate combustorum. 1710. pp.[16]. [25.]

JEAN BAPTISTE HANNOT, Index librorum prohibitorum, ex magno indice romano et appendice unica fideliter excerptus. Namurci 1714. pp.xxvi. 276. [1750.]

— — Index ou Catalogue des principaux livres

condamnés et defendus par l'Église. Namur 1714.
pp.[xxxviii].xxxii.430.18. [2500.]

JOHANN CHRISTOPH WENDLER, De libris a pontificiis aliisqve hæreticis in præjudicium doctrinæ
purioris nostra et superiore ætate suppressis et
corruptis schediasma. Jenæ 1714. pp.[iv].20.32
[*sic*, 40].66. [100.]
reissued in 1730.

CATALOGUE des ouvrages mis à l'index, contenant le nom de tous les livres condamnés par la
cour de Rome, depuis l'invention de l'imprimerie
jusqu'en 1825, avec les dates des décrets de leur
condamnation. . . . Seconde édition. 1826. pp.[ii].
lxi.361. [7000.]

FR. HEINRICH REUSCH, Die indices librorum
prohibitorum des sechzehnten jahrhunderts gesammelt und herausgegeben. Literarischer verein
in Stuttgart: Bibliothek (vol.clxxvi): Tübingen
1886. pp.[iv].598. [10,000.]

A[BRAHAM ADOLF] BERLINER, Censur und con-
fiscation hebräischer bücher im Kirchenstaate.
Auf grund der inquisitions-akten in der Vaticana
und Vallicellana dargestellt. Frankfurt a. M. 1891.
pp.[ii].65. [1250.]

JOSEPH HILGERS, Der index der verbotenen

bücher. In seiner neuen fassung dargelegt und rechtlich-historisch gewürdigt. Freiburg i. B. 1904. pp.xxi.638. [5000.]

JOSEPH HILGERS, Die bücherverbote in papstbriefen. Kanonistisch-bibliographische studie. Freiburg i. B. 1907. pp.viii.107. [250.]

ALBERT SLEUMER, Index romanus. Verzeichnis sämtlicher auf dem römischen index stehenden deutschen bücher, desgleichen aller wichtigen fremdsprachlichen bücher seit dem jahre 1750.... Vierte . . . auflage. Osnabrück 1909. pp.132. [1250.]
— — Elfte . . . auflage. 1956. pp.220. [2750.]

Erotica. [*see also* **Condemned books** *and* **Scatology.**]

[GUSTAV FRIEDRICH KLEMM], Verzeichniss einer sammlung gut gehaltener, grösstentheils sehr seltener erotischer und sotadischer schriften. Dresden 1834. pp.[ii].76. [1250.]

the collection was that of Carl Gottlob Günther.

[JULES GAY], Bibliographie des principaux ouvrages relatifs à l'amour, aux femmes, au mariage. . . . Par m. le c. d'I.*** 1861. pp.viii.150. [3000.]

— Seconde édition. 1864. pp.xi.coll.810. [7000.]

a copy in the British museum contains ms. additions by Henry Spencer Ashbee.

—— 3me édition. Turin &c. 1871–1873. pp. xvi.432 + [iii].468 + [iii].468 + [iii].470 + [iii].472 + [iii].168[*sic*, 468]. [20,000.]

also issued with Nice and San Remo imprints.

—— Quatrième édition, entièrement refondue . . . par J. Lemonnyer. 1894–1900. pp.viii.coll.928 + pp.[iii].coll.960 + [iii].coll.1408 + pp.[v].1300. [35,000.]

J[OHANN] G[EORG THEODOR] GRAESSE, Notice sur

les écrivains érotiques du quinzième siècle et du commencement du seizième. Extrait de l'ouvrage allemand... 'Histoire universelle de la littérature'. Traduit et annoté par un bibliophile français. Bruxelles 1865. pp.81. [250.]

ARTHUR [MARTIN] DINAUX, Les sociétés badines, bachiques, littéraires et chantantes. Leur histoire et leurs travaux.... Revu et classé par m. Gustave Brunet. 1867. pp.vi.459+[iii].410. [1000.]

CATALOGUE d'une collection de livres curieux, facéties, érotiques . . . provenant de la bibliothèque d'un amateur distingué m. S.... de S.... Dresden 1875. pp.19. [630.]

H. NAY [*pseud.* HUGO HAYN], Bibliotheca Germanorum erotica. Verzeichniss der gesammten deutschen erotischen literatur. Leipzig 1875. pp. [iv].152. [3750.]

— — Zweite ... auflage. ... Von Hugo Hayn. 1885. pp.iv.484. [9000.]

— — [another edition, by Hugo Hayn and Alfred N. Gotendorf (vol.ix: Paul English)]. Bibliotheca Germanorum erotica & curiosa. München 1912–1929. pp.vi.716+715+648+566 +520+586+734+682+viii.668. [70,000.]

L. C[ONSTANTIN], Catalogue des tableaux, livres
. . . composant le cabinet de m. L. C. 1876. pp.70.
[212.]

[HENRY SPENCER ASHBEE], Index librorum prohibitorum: being notes bio- biblio- iconographical and critical, on curious and uncommon
books. By Pisanus Fraxi. 1877. pp.lxxvi.543. [500.]
250 copies privately printed; facsimiles were issued
London 1960 and New York 1962.

[ANTOINE LAPORTE], Bibliographie clérico-
galante. Ouvrages galants ou singuliers sur
l'amour, les femmes, le mariage, le théâtre, etc.
écrits par des abbés, prêtres, chanoines, religieux,
religieuses, évêques, archevêques, cardinaux et
papes. Par l'apôtre bibliographe. 1879. pp.xxviii.
178. [1000.]

[HENRY SPENCER ASHBEE], Centuria librorum
absconditorum: being notes bio- biblio- iconographical and critical on curious and uncommon
books. By Pisanus Fraxi. 1879. pp.lx.596. [500.]
250 copies privately printed; facsimiles were issued
London 1960 and New York 1962.

[ANTOINE LAPORTE], La bibliographie jaune. . . .
Par l'apôtre bibliographe. Cocupolis [Paris] 1880.
pp.[iii].106. [400.]

a bibliography of cukoldry; the dedication is signed 'J.-Joseph Cornutus'.

CATALOGUE de livres rares et curieux sur l'amour, les femmes et le mariage, faisant partie du cabinet d'un bibliophile suédois [count Kristoffer Rutger Ludvig Manderström]. Stockholm 1883–1884. pp.vii.40+[iv].90. [1155.]

[SIR WILLIAM LAIRD CLOWES], Bibliotheca arcana seu catalogus librorum penetralium, being brief notices of books that have been secretly printed, prohibited by law, seized, anathematised, burnt or bowdlerised. By Speculator morum. [1884–]1885. pp.[ii].xxii.142.xxvi. [630.]

[HENRY SPENCER ASHBEE], Catena librorum tacendorum: being notes bio- biblio- iconographical and critical, on curious and uncommon books. By Pisanus Fraxi. 1885. pp.lx.596. [500.]
250 copies privately printed; facsimiles were issued London 1960 and New York 1962.

HUGO HAYN, Bibliotheca Germanorum gynaecologica et cosmetica . . . unter besonderer berücksichtigung der älteren populären medicin. Leipzig 1886. pp.[iii].158. [3000.]

HUGO HAYN, Bibliotheca erotica et curiosa

monacensis. Verzeichnis französischer, italienischer, spanischer, englischer, holländischer und neulateinischer erotica und curiosa, von welchen keine deutschen uebersetzungen bekannt sind. Zusammengestellt auf der Königl. hof- und staats-bibliothek zu München. Berlin 1889. pp. [viii].86. [628.]

[CARL FRIEDRICH WEGENER], Vorschlag zu einer lesebibliothek für junge frauenzimmer. Ein bibliographisch-erotisches curiosum . . . mit . . . einem verzeichniss scherzhafter catalogi . . . herausgegeben von Hugo Hayn. Borna 1889. pp.63. [47.]
reprinted from the author's Raritäten *(1778–1785), vi.102–145.*

ENFER du grenier. Lille [printed] [1891]. pp.23. [100.]

FORBIDDEN books. By an old bibliophile. Paris 1902. pp.xii.83. [30.]
250 copies privately printed.

HUGO HAYN, Vier neue curiositäten-bibliographieen. . . . Bibliotheca selecta erotico-curiosa dresdensis. Jena 1905. pp.57–88. [300.]
describes books in the Königliche öffentliche bibliothek, Dresden.

GUILLAUME APOLLINAIRE [*pseud.* WILHELM KOSTROWITSKY], FERNAND FLEURET and LOUIS PERCEAU,

L'enfer de la Bibliothèque nationale. Icono-bio-bibliographie. 1913. pp.416. [930.]
— — Nouvelle édition. 1919. pp.415.
a typewritten supplement up to 1934, edited by Alfred Rose, is in the British museum.

HUGO HAYN and ALFRED N. GOTENDORF, Floh-litteratur (de pulicibus) des in- und auslandes, vom XVI. jahrhundert bis zur neuzeit. [*s.l.*] 1913. pp.[ii].36. [200.]
a copy in the Bodleian library contains numerous ms. notes by John Hodgkin.

BERNHARD STERN–SZANA, Bibliotheca curiosa et erotica. Beschreibung meiner sammlung. [Vienna 1921]. pp.247. [264.]
privately printed.

FERNANDO BRUNER PRIETO, Infierno de la biblioteca Villalonga. Icono-bio-bibliografía de las obras que componen esta colección. Palma de Mallorca 1923. pp.xx.77. [173.]

ALFRED K. VON TRELDEWEHR, Der privatdruck. Erster katalog erotischer mappen, bilder u. bücher. [*s.l.*] 1924. pp.15.16. [71.]

LOUIS PERCEAU, Bibliographie du roman érotique au XIXᵉ siècle, donnant une description complète de tous les romans, nouvelles, et autres ouvrages en prose, publiés sous le manteau en français, de 1800 à nos jours, et de toutes leurs réimpressions. 1930. pp.401 + 417. [870.]

ERNST DAHN, Verbotene und undeutsche bücher. Ein führer zur völkischen gestaltung der deutschen leihbüchereien. Berlin 1933. pp.19. [600.]

ROLF S. READE [*pseud.* ALFRED ROSE], Registrum librorum eroticorum vel (sub hac specie) dubiorum: Opus bibliographicum et praecipue bibliothecariis destinatum. 1936. pp.[iv].xii.204+[iii]. 205–398. [4000.]
200 copies privately printed.

[CHARLES FREDERICK HEARTMAN], The 'blue book'. A bibliographical attempt to describe the guide books to the houses of ill fame in New Orleans. . . . By Semper idem. Heartman's historical series (no.50): [*s.l.*] 1936. pp.3–77. [13.]
privately printed.

MAX IVERSEN and ÅSE HENRIKSEN, Forbudte bøger. To aarhundreders beslaglagte og konfiskerede værker. En annoteret bibliografi. København 1948. pp.199. [200.]
500 copies printed.

Erotica

HERBERT E[DWARD] STANTON, Censor's choice: a checklist of banned books. Delray Beach, Fla., 1953. ff.2. [75.]★

LISTE générale des ouvrages, publications et revues françaises et étrangères interdits . . . à la vente . . . à l'affichage. Corporation des bouquinistes: [1963]. pp.45. [2000.]

Forged books.

[*under this heading are included bibliographies of books with false or imaginary imprints, and of pirated books.*]

JOHANN MICHAEL REINELIUS, Dissertatio philosophica de plagio literario. Lipsiæ [1673]. pp. [271]. [1000.]

— — Nunc recusa & sex accessionibus locupletata. Levcopetræ [Accessiones: Jenæ] 1679. pp. [iii].282+72. [1000.]

[EMIL OTTOKAR WELLER], Katalog der seit dem 17. jahrhunderte bis auf die neueste zeit unter falscher firma erschienenen schriften. Zweite . . . auflage. Leipzig 1850. pp.60. [900.]

EMIL WELLER, Die falschen und fingirten druckorte. . . . Zugleich als der 'Maskirten literatur' zweither theil. Leipzig 1858. pp.vii.200. [7000.]

— — Neue nachtraege zum Index pseudonymorum und zu den Falschen und fingirten druckorten 1862. pp.iv.74. [350.]

— — Zweite . . . auflage. 1864.

i. Die deutschen und lateinischen schriften.

pp.viii.333. [6000.]

ii. Die französischen schriften. pp.vii.310. [6000.]

a facsimile of this edition, with Nachträge, *was issued Hildesheim 1961.*

[PIERRE] GUSTAVE BRUNET, Imprimeurs imaginaires et libraires supposés. Étude bibliographique, suivie de recherches sur quelques ouvrages imprimés avec des indications fictives de lieux ou avec des dates singulières. 1866. pp.[iii].290. [2500.]

a facsimile reprint was published, New York 1962.

OCTAVE [JOSEPH] DELEPIERRE, Supercheries littéraires, pastiches, suppositions d'auteur, dans les lettres et dans les arts. Londres 1872. pp.[viii].328. [100.] ·

ROBERT [MARIE] REBOUL, Anonymes, pseudonymes et supercheries littéraires de la Provence, ancienne et moderne. Marseille 1878. pp.447. [2355.]

100 copies printed.

[PIERRE GUSTAVE BRUNET], Recherches sur les imprimeries imaginaires, clandestines et particulières. . . . Par . . . Philomneste junior. Bruxelles 1879. pp.viii.13[*sic*, 113]. [500.]

ARTHUR BOITTE, Bibliographie des ouvrages français contrefaits en Belgique dans le format in-32 et connus sous le nom de collection Laurent. Bruxelles 1882. pp.75. [300.]

500 copies printed.

[PIERRE] G[USTAVE] BRUNET, Les supercheries typographiques. Essai bibliographique. Bordeaux [printed] [1884]. pp.20. [50.]

LIST of references on literary forgeries. Library of Congress: Washington 1923. ff.4. [35.]*

SÉAMUS Ó CASAIDE, Fictitious imprints on books printed in Ireland. Bibliographical society of Ireland (vol.iii, no.4): Wexford [printed] 1927. pp.[ii].31–36. [35.]

FACSIMILES & forgeries. A guide to a timely exhibition. William L. Clements library: Bulletin (no.xxi): Ann Arbor 1934. pp.[ii].14. [50.]

FANNIE E[LIZABETH] RATCHFORD, Certain nineteenth century forgeries. An exhibition of books and letters at the university of Texas. [Austin 1946]. pp.57. [100.]

MARINO PARENTI, Dizionario dei luoghi di stampa falsi, inventati o supposti in opere di autori e traduttori italiani, con un'appendice sulla data "Italia" e un saggio sui falsi luoghi italiani usati all'estero, o in Italia, da autori stranieri. Biblioteca bibliografica italica (no.1): Firenze 1951. pp. 312. [2500.]

VARIOUS extraordinary books procured by Thomas J. Wise and now displayed on All fools day in observance of the centenary of his birth. University of Texas: Humanities research center: [Austin] 1959. pp.18. [169.]

300 copies printed.

Miniature books.

[PIERRE BENJAMIN] DE LA FAYE, Catalogue complet des républiques imprimées en Hollande in-16. 1842. pp.48. [100.]

— — Nouvelle édition. 1854. pp.48. [100.]

[CHARLES ANTOINE BRISSART-BINET], Cazin, marchand libraire rémois. Essai sur sa vie et ses éditions. Par un Cazinophile. Reims 1859. pp.12. [15.]

[—] — [another edition]. Cazin, sa vie et ses éditions. Cazinopolis [Reims] 1863. pp.245. [300.]
320 copies printed.

[—] — Réimpression de l'édition de 1863. [Edited by A. Brissat and Auguste Maille]. Cazinopolis [Châlons-sur-Marne]. 1876. pp.267. [300.]

WILLIAM E[DWARD] A[RMYTAGE] AXON, The smallest books in the world: a bibliographical note. Manchester [1876]. pp.6. [25.]
privately printed.

[A. CORROËNNE], Manuel du Cazinophile. Le petit-format à figures, collection parisienne in-18

(vraie collection de Cazin). 1878. pp.[iii].180.
[500.]

LOUIS MOHR, Des impressions microscopiques.
1879. pp.11. [40.]
100 copies printed.

A. CORROËNNE, Période initiale du petit format
à vignettes et figures. Collection Cazin. Bulletin
du Cazinophile: 1880. pp.[iii].240. [30.]
377 copies printed.

CH[ARLES] NAUROY, Bibliographie des impressions microscopiques. 1881. pp.128. [750.]
250 copies printed.

ARNOLD KUCZYŃSKI, Verzeichniss einer sammlung mikroskopischer drucke und formate im
besitze von Albert Brockhaus. Leipzig 1888. pp.
vi.42. [98.]

GEORG FRICK, Die elzevir'schen republiken.
Halle a. S. 1892. pp.[ii].34. [50.]

CATALOGUE de la collection d'éditions microscopiques de madame G. P. 1893. pp.35.
50 copies privately printed.

[A. CORROËNNE], Livres-bijoux, précurseurs des
Cazins. Biblio-iconographie historique des premières collections fondées de 1773 à 1779 à Lille,

à Lyon et à Orléans. [1894]. pp.108. [100.]
also issued as the first series of Les petits joyaux
bibliophiliques.

[A. CORROËNNE], Icono-mono-bibliographie des
petits formats in-24 du 18ᵉ siècle. Collection de
Lyon. [1894]. pp.[iii].72. [80.]
400 copies printed.

GASTIN TISSANDIER, Livres minuscules. La plus
grande bibliothèque des plus petits livres du
monde: collection de m. Georges Salomon. 1894.
pp.20. [50.]

A SHORT list of microscopic books in the library
of the Grolier club, mostly preserved by Samuel
P[utnam] Avery. New York 1911. pp.[iii].121–
152. [176.]

KARL J. LÜTHI, Bücher kleinsten formates.
Bibliothek des Schweizerbibliophilen (1st ser.,
vol.i): Bern 1924. pp.[vii].47. [25.]
250.copies printed.

A. TÜNEEWA, Miniaturausgaben und die kollek-
tion solcher in der Öffentlichen staatsbibliothek.
Odessa: Öffentliche staatsbibliothek: Leipzig 1926.
pp.[ii].21. [200.]
250 copies printed.

Miniature Books

DOUGLAS C[RAWFORD] MCMURTRIE, Miniature incunabula. Chicago 1929. pp.11. [6.]
250 copies privately printed.

[P. E. SPIELMANN], Catalogue of the library of miniature books collected by Percy Edwin Spielmann. [1961]. pp.xv.289. [525.]
500 copies printed.

Special Subjects

Biblioteca nazionale Vittorio Emanuele III.

[GUERRIERA GUERRIERI], Cenno storico-bibliografico della biblioteca. Reale biblioteca nazionale Vittorio Emanuele III: Quaderni (ser.II, no.I). Napoli 1940. pp.31. [29.]

Bibliothèque nationale, Paris.

ÉMILE PIERRET, Inventaire détaillé des catalogues usuels de la Bibliothèque nationale. 1889. pp.31. [125.]

É[MILE] PIERRET, Essai d'une bibliographie historique de la Bibliothèque nationale. 1892. pp.161. [617.]

LÉON VALLÉE, La Bibliothèque nationale. Choix de documents pour servir à l'histoire de l'établissement et de ses collections. 1894. pp.xii.526. [1342.]

SUZANNE DUPUY, État sommaire des catalogues de la Bibliothèque nationale actuellement en usage. 1933. pp.44. [316.]

LES CATALOGUES imprimés de la Bibliothèque

nationale. Liste, description, contenu. 1943. pp. 205. [460.]

—— [another edition]. 1953. pp.204.xxvii. [561.]

CATALOGUES et publications en vente. Bibliothèque nationale: 1962. pp.51. [262.]

Bibliotherapy.

BIBLIOTHERAPY. A bibliography, 1900–1952. Veterans administration: Medical & general reference library: Washington 1952. pp.[ii].18. [378.]*

Bodleian library.

THE BODLEIAN library in the seventeenth century. Guide to an exhibition. Oxford 1951. pp.53. [157.]

Brașov.

JULIUS GROSS, Kronstädter drucke 1535–1886. Ein beitrag zur kulturgeschichte Kronstadts. Kronstadt 1886. pp.ix.197. [1750.]

Cataloguing, library.

TORSTEIN [KNUTSON TORSTENSEN-] JAHR and ADAM JULIUS STROHM, Bibliography of cooperativecataloguing and the printing of catalogue cards, with incidental references to international bibliography and the universal catalogue. Washington 1903. pp.116. [366.]

[ALBERTO VILLALÓN], Catalogación y clasificación. Libros y folletos, publicaciones aparecidas hasta 1948 inclusive. Colección bibliografías y lecturas bibliotécnicas (ser. B, group 1, vol.i): Santiago de Chile 1951. pp.xxiv.76. [325.]

KEITARO AMANO, A bibliography on cataloguing of western books in Japan (tentative). [*s.l.*] 1959. ff.[iii].16. [150.]*

Classification, library.

CLASSIFICATION. Summer school of library service: Aberystwyth 1922. pp.[7]. [42.]

[ALBERTO VILLALÓN], Catalogación y clasificación. Libros y folletos, publicaciones aparecidas hasta 1948 inclusive. Colección bibliografías y lecturas bibliotécnicas (ser. B, group 1, vol.i): Santiago de Chile 1951. pp.xxiv.76. [325.]

A FIRST list of serial in which articles are classified by the universal decimal classification. Science library: Bibliographical series (no.760): [1958]. pp.3. [100.]*

— A second list. . . . (no.770): 1959. single leaf. [10.]*

PAULE SALVAN, Les classifications. Guide bibliographique sommaire. 1961. ff.13. [64.]*

Cotta'sche buchhandlung.

JUBILÄUMS-KATALOG der J. G. Cotta'schen buchhandlung nachfolger, 1659–1909. Stuttgart &c. [1910]. pp.lii.coll.408. [3500.]

Drukarnia narodowa.

DRUKARNIA narodowa w Krakowie 1895–1935. Krakowie [1935]. pp.282.cxxviii. [3500.]

Encyclopedias.

A LIST of cyclopedias and dictionaries, with a list of directories. John Crerar library: Chicago 1904. pp.iv.272. [1600.]

СЛОВАРИ и энциклопедии за 1918–1943 гг. Государственная публичная библиотека: Научно-библиографический отдел: Москва 1944. pp.60.

КАТАЛОГ энциклопедической и справочной литературы. Институт по изучению СССР:

Сообщения библиотеки института (no.7): Мюнхен 1955. pp.42. [500.]*

ROBERT L. UNDERBRINK, About encyclopedias. An annotated bibliography [Jacksonville, Ill. 1960]. pp.[ii].11. [80.]

I[SAAK] M[IKHAILOVICH] KAUFMAN, Русские энциклопедии. Государственная ... библиотека СССР имени В. И. Ленина: Москва 1960. pp.104. [40.]

I. V. GUDOVSHCHIKOVA, Общие зарубежные энциклопедии. Ленинградский государственный библиотечный институт имени Н. К. Крупской: Ленинград 1963. pp.87. [70.]

GENERAL encyclopedias in print. Reference books research service: Akron, O. 1963. pp.48. [34.]

Encyclopedists. [*see also* **Denis Diderot**.]

L'ENCYCLOPÉDIE et les encyclopédistes. Exposition organisée par le Centre international de synthèse. Bibliothèque nationale: 1932. pp.84. [298.]

Facsimiles.

[ÉMILE A. VAN MOÉ], Trois cents chefs-d'œuvre en fac-similé. Manuscrits, enluminures, livres précieux [&c.]. Bibliothèque nationale: 1940. pp.iv. 52. [300.]

Indexes. [*see also* **Periodical publications.**]

NORMA OLIN IRELAND, An index to indexes. A subject bibliography of published indexes. Useful reference series (no.67): Boston 1942. pp.iii–xvi.107. [1000.]

NORMA OLIN IRELAND, Local indexes in american libraries. A union list of unpublished indexes. Boston 1947. pp.221. [2500.]

Library of Congress.

LIST of references on the Library of Congress. Library of Congress: Washington 1916. ff.3. [43.]★

PUBLICATIONS by members of the Library staff, Jan. 1. 1942–June 30, 1943. Library of Congress: Washington [1943]. ff.24. [330.]★

PUBLICATIONS of the Library of Congress: a representative list. Library of Congress: Washington 1949. ff.7. [48.]★

LIBRARY of Congress publications in print. Library of Congress: Washington 1952. pp.iv.77. [565.]★

— [supplement]. pp.13. [95.]★

THE LIBRARY of Congress. A selected list of references. Library of Congress: Washington 1956. pp.vi.20. [142.]*

Livres à clef.

CH[ARLES] NODIER, De quelques livres satyriques et de leur clef. Bulletin du bibliophile (nos.9, 11, suppléments): [1834]. pp.11+11. [34.]

J[OSEPH] M[ARIE] QUÉRARD, Livres à clef. Œuvres posthumes . . . publiés par [Pierre] G[ustave] Brunet: Bordeaux 1873. pp.[iii].112+[iii].113–224. [125.]

300 copies printed.

FERNAND DRUJON, Les livres à clef. Étude de bibliographie critique et analytique. [1885–]1888. pp.xvi.coll.674 + pp.[iii].coll.675–1311.pp.1312–1357. [1250.]

EARLE [FRANCIS] WALBRIDGE, Literary characters drawn from life, "romans à clef", "drames à clef", real people in poetry. New York 1936. pp.192. [1000.]

— — Index and key . . . prepared by the class in advanced reference, 1936–37, of the university of Illinois library school. 1938. pp.32. [1500.]

— — Supplement 1936–1953. [1953]. pp.31. [1500.]

GEORG SCHNEIDER, Die schlüsselliteratur. Stuttgart 1951–1953. pp.xvi.214 + viii.212 + x.189. [1000.]

Longmans & co.

CHARLES JAMES LONGMAN, The house of Longman, 1724–1800. A bibliographical history. 1936. pp.xv.488. [2250.]

500 copies printed.

Lübeck, Stadtbibliothek.

HERMANN A. STOLTERFOHT, Bibliographie zur geschichte der Lübecker stadtbibliothek. Stadtbibliothek der freien und Hansestadt Lübeck: Veröffentlichungen (vol.iii, part 1): Lübeck 1929. pp.71. [700.]

MacLehose, James.

BOOKS published by James MacLehose from 1838 to 1881 and by James MacLehose and sons to 1905, presented to the library of the university of Glasgow. Glasgow 1905. pp.vii.63. [578.]

Macmillan & co.

[JAMES FOSTER], A bibliographical catalogue of Macmillan and co.'s publications from 1843 to 1889. 1891. pp.vii.715. [5000.]

Microfilms, microcards.

BLANCHE PRICHARD MCCRUM, Microfilms and microcards: their use in research. A selected list of references. Library of Congress: General reference and bibliography division: Washington 1949. pp.19. [77.]*

— — [another edition]. 1950. pp.[ii].v.81. [263.]*

Palimpsests.

FRIDEGARIUS MONE, De libris palimpsestris tam latinis quam graecis. Carlsruhae 1855. pp.62. [150.]

Public record office.

'MEANS of reference'. [Public record office: 1938]. pp.8. [43.]

Punched card systems.

WALTER LINGENBERG, Über die anwendung von lochkartenverfahren in bibliotheken. Arbeiten aus dem Bibliothekar-lehrinstitut des landes Nord-rhein-Westfalen (no.9): Köln 1955. pp.85. [200.]

MARTIN SCHEELE [and FRANZ HODES], Literatur über lochkartenverfahren. Schlitz/Hessen 1959. pp.116. [1999.]

Radcliffe library.

BIBLIOTHECA radcliviana, 1749–1949. Catalogue of an exhibition. Oxford 1949. pp.47. [100.]

Rascher und Cie.

MAX RASCHER, 25 Jahre verlagstätigkeit des Rascher und c^ie a. g., 1908–1933. Ein katalog. Zürich &c. 1933. pp.[iii].160. [2200.]

Union catalogues.

ARTHUR BERTHOLD, Union catalogues. A selective bibliography. Union library catalogue of the Philadelphia metropolitan area: Philadelphia 1936. pp.xvi.70. [356.]*

Vaticana, Bibliotheca apostolica.

[ACHILLE RATTI], Pubblicazioni della biblioteca apostolica Vaticana. Roma 1915. pp.188. [400.]

I LIBRI editi dalla biblioteca Vaticana, MDCCCLXXXV–MCMXLVII. Catalogo ragionato e illustrato. Città del Vaticano 1947. pp.187. [250.]
— The books published by the Vatican library

[&c. Translated by Mary E. Stanley]. Vatican city 1947. pp.iii–liv.187. [250.]

GIULIO BATTELLI, *ed.* Bibliografia dell'Archivo vaticano. Città del Vaticano 1962–1963. pp.xix. 855+iii–xix.951. [20,000.]*

Wells, Gabriel.

[CHARLES FREDERICK HEARTMAN], Bibliography of the writings and speeches of Gabriel Wells. Hattiesburg, Mo. 1939. pp.24. [200.]
    'less than' 200 copies privately printed.

William L. Clements library.

THE WILLIAM L. CLEMENTS library. A brief description and bibliographical record 1923–1944. William L. Clements library: Bulletin (no.xliii): Ann Arbor 1944. pp.47. [250.]